T0102187

JUST A
SPRITZ

JUST A SPRITZ

57 Simple Sparkling Sips with Low to No Alcohol

DANIELLE CENTONI

Photographs by Eric Medsker

ARTISAN | NEW YORK

Copyright © 2022 by Danielle Centoni
Photographs copyright © 2022 by Eric Medsker

All rights reserved. No portion of this book may be reproduced—
mechanically, electronically, or by any other means, including
photocopying—without written permission of the publisher.

Library of Congress Cataloging-in-Publication Data
Names: Centoni, Danielle, author.
Title: Just a spritz / Danielle Centoni ; photographs by Eric Medsker.
Description: New York, NY : Artisan, a division of
Workman Publishing Co., Inc. [2022] | Includes index.
Identifiers: LCCN 2021034946 | ISBN 9781579659974
Subjects: LCSH: Spritzes (Cocktails) | Nonalcoholic beverages. |
LCGFT: Cookbooks.
Classification: LCC TX951 .C39 2021 | DDC 641.87/4—dc23
LC record available at https://lccn.loc.gov/2021034946

Cover design by Headcase Design
Interior design by Nina Simoneaux

Artisan books are available at special discounts when purchased in bulk for
premiums and sales promotions as well as for fund-raising or educational
use. Special editions or book excerpts also can be created to specification.
For details, contact the Special Sales Director at the address below, or send
an e-mail to specialmarkets@workman.com.

For speaking engagements, contact speakersbureau@workman.com.

Published by Artisan
A division of Workman Publishing Co., Inc.
225 Varick Street
New York, NY 10014-4381
artisanbooks.com

Artisan is a registered trademark of Workman Publishing Co., Inc.

Printed in China on responsibly sourced paper
First printing, April 2022

1 3 5 7 9 10 8 6 4 2

CONTENTS

PREFACE

ALONE IN FLORENCE, after a day of wandering through museums and shops, I stopped into a café on a quiet plaza just as the afternoon sun had started to wane. I ordered a drink and pulled out a book, ready to settle in for a bit before figuring out my next move. Soon the waiter brought me a little ham sandwich complete with frilly toothpick. Oh, shoot. Had he misheard me? Had I said the wrong thing? Thirty seconds later he was back, no doubt to pick up the misdelivered sandwich. No, he set down a bowl of potato chips and a small dish of olives and walked away. Now I was starting to panic. What to do? Just as I was trying to figure out how to explain that I'd ordered a cocktail, not a meal, he was back, this time with the drink, setting it down with a nod and smile. That's when the light went off. Oh, yes! I'd heard about this—aperitivo.

To say I was smitten is an understatement. A light cocktail and a few salty snacks just for me. It was like an open invitation to relax. Not so much booze or food that my night would end there; just enough to send me on my way. I've enjoyed my fair share of happy hours at bars in the States, but that often felt like bargain hunting for dinner, trying to score the biggest portions at the lowest prices. Aperitivo is different.

It's a tradition that stuck with me even after I returned home. Sure, my husband and I don't make time for it every night, but we relish those evenings when I prepare a little plate of olives and maybe a few slices of cheese and salumi, and mix up a couple of spritzes to enjoy on the porch before switching to dinner prep. It's the best way to shake off the grind of the workday.

And I'm not the only one who thinks so. This low-alcohol dinnertime preamble has started catching on beyond Italy's borders—especially its fizzy, refreshing, bracingly bitter mascot, the Aperol spritz. Although a spritz can be made with any bitter liqueur, plus sparkling wine, a splash of soda water, and ice, the version from Veneto, the Italian region where Aperol was born, has become the de facto spritz all over Europe and the United States, first gaining a foothold in the States in 2017 and rocketing to popularity and Instagram ubiquity within just a year. At the same time, sparkling wine, an integral spritz component, was enjoying its fifteenth consecutive year of steady growth in consumption, even shedding its "pinkies up" persona and finding its way into cans. Clearly, the spritz has struck a chord, and it's here to stay.

But the Aperol spritz is just a drop in a sea of bubbly possibilities, and that's where this book comes in. It's packed with dozens of effervescent sippers that are easy to make, easy to drink, and easy on the budget. No matter what flavor you're craving, no matter if it's a hot August night or a blustery January evening, there's a drink in these pages tailor-made to give you a taste of that effortless aperitivo life, any night of the week. Think of these recipes as your road map to relaxation. So set down the phone, put on some tunes, pop the cork, and spritz the day away.

INTRODUCTION

T AKE AN INTENSELY FLAVORED and usually bitter liqueur, tame it with a big glug of sparkling wine, then lighten it up with a splash of bubbly water and a handful of ice. That, in a nutshell, is the spritz—the most refreshing, laid-back, intrinsically forgiving, and nearly effortless low-alcohol drink in the cocktail kingdom.

Since spritzes are low ABV (alcohol by volume), they'll keep you on your feet (or at least in your lounge chair). As with a "session" beer, you can drink a couple in one sitting and still carry on with your evening with no regrets the next morning. And for those occasions when you don't want any alcohol at all, this book includes zero-proof variations and stand-alone recipes with all of the flavor and none of the buzz.

You don't need any special tools or behind-the-bar know-how to make a spritz at home. Simultaneously simple to make and ripe for creativity, the spritz is the ideal platform for both budding cocktail enthusiasts and longtime aficionados who want to experiment. Although it's entirely possible to build a repertoire of recipes based on DIY tinctures and obscure small-batch spirits, the spritz is meant to be an easy-breezy drink, so you won't find complicated concoctions in these pages. We'll leave that to the pros who have a library of spirits to play with and a team of barbacks at their beck and call.

This book aims to satisfy a craving for a refreshingly fizzy adult drink, preferably with as little time and effort as possible. It includes a few fun homemade syrups and tart shrubs for when you have some time on your hands, but otherwise the drinks don't require any advance planning at all. Each recipe serves one—no cocktail party required—but most are easy to scale up if you're having company.

While many cocktail books are organized by spirit or style, this one is organized by flavor, and each flavor gets its own chapter, so whatever you're in the mood for, you can zero right in to satisfy your desire. It starts with classic spritz recipes, because once you get a taste for those, you can really start riffing. Then you'll find drinks with a floral touch, ideal for spring brunches or breezy afternoons. Next up, recipes that showcase juicy, summery fruits like berries, melons, and peaches, followed by drinks that highlight bright, tangy citrus and tropical flavors. Spritzes that put bitter, herbal flavors front and center are next, and they're fabulous with salty snacks any time of year. Finally, the holiday chapter offers a lineup with an emphasis on fall and winter flavors like apples, cranberries, baking spices, and toasty nuts. Even though many of the recipes offer a spirits-free variation, at the end of every chapter is a nonalcoholic spritz that shines on its own.

Most of the recipes were created in the Italian tradition, riffing on the original Venetian spritz and its sacred trinity of a bitter liqueur, bubbly wine, and fizzy soda water, with juices and syrups splashed in for variety and fun. That means almost all have a "backbone," an edge of bitterness that keeps the drink from tasting like pop. It also means they're perfect for whetting the appetite before dinner, just as the Italians intended.

Although some of the liqueurs might seem obscure to the uninitiated, they're all pretty easy to find—and that's intentional. This is a book for us regular folk. No intricate infusions. No spirits you need a passport to get. And it uses a limited number of bottles, so you don't have to go broke trying out more than a few recipes. What it does have are more than fifty wildly different takes on not-too-boozy, bittersweet bubbles, enough to keep you spritzing all year long.

The Allure of Italy's Aperitivo Hour

The word *aperitivo* is derived from the Latin *aperire*, which means "to open." And that's really what aperitivo in Italy is—an opener to the evening, a few snacks and a drink to ease the transition from day to night. It's similar to happy hour in the States, but in Italy, aperitivo is generally more refined. It's not about filling up on the cheap; it's about relaxing.

It's also traditionally more of a northern Italian thing, like spritzes themselves, and every big city, bar, or café in the region has its own way of doing aperitivo. Some have a few set snacks that come automatically with your drink (which doesn't have to be a spritz, by the way), some lay out a buffet of handheld foods, and some offer a tight menu of bites to choose from. Of course, some of the offerings are better than others, but the spirit of the aperitivo remains the same—a little time, space, and refreshment to get a second wind.

WHAT EXACTLY IS A SPRITZ?

There are countless ways to make a fizzy cocktail, but they can't all be called a spritz. At its most basic, a spritz is a glass of wine lightened up with a splash of water. That's how the modern versions all started. Austrian soldiers stationed in northern Italy in the 1800s couldn't stomach the local wine, so they diluted it with a *Spritz* (German for "spray" or "splash") of still water. By the early twentieth century, people were subbing in far more refreshing bubbly soda water, and soon after began to play around with amari (Italian bitter liqueurs) instead of just wine.

While Italy holds regional affinities for specific amari, there are no such allegiances in the States. Now that the spritz has become part of the American mixological lexicon (and, thanks to the global popularity of the Aperol spritz, is no longer solely associated with the low-cal white wine "spritzers" of the 1980s), bartenders have taken the format and run with it. These days a spritz can incorporate all manner of spirits, whether they're from the French Alps or an artisan producer on the West Coast, and often includes modern touches like muddled fruits, infused syrups, and bubbles that go far beyond wine.

A spritz can be made with almost any bubbly and any spirit, but to keep it true to form, a spritz must be:

- low in alcohol
- bubbly
- refreshing

- at least a little bit bitter
- the opposite of fussy

Refreshment is the name of the game. That's why classic spritzes are built with liqueurs, not high-proof spirits. And in Italy, the birthplace of the spritz, those liqueurs are usually very bitter. Why? Because spritzes are meant to be a predinner drink. Bitter compounds stimulate the taste receptors on the tongue and spark the appetite for the dinner to come (see page 119). If you haven't experienced the magic of cooking dinner with a spritz in hand, you're missing out.

GET TO KNOW THE KEY PLAYERS

Building the perfect spritz bar doesn't require a liquor store's worth of bottles, and it doesn't require deep pockets either. You need only a few key bottles to make a multitude of drinks, and the necessary liqueurs and vermouths are typically far cheaper than full-proof spirits. As for the sparkling wine, you can find a favorite and just stick to it, or have fun exploring a wide range of bubblies. Here's the lowdown on the essentials.

Something Bitter

A spritz isn't really a spritz without at least a hint of mouthwatering bitterness. Italian amari (bitter liqueurs) like citrusy Aperol and Campari, or richly spiced Averna and Cynar, are classic choices. But that's just the beginning. Herbal aromatized wines like red (sweet) and white (dry) vermouths, floral liqueurs like St-Germain, and even high-proof spirits like rum can form the basis of a spritz. No one expects you to buy them all, especially since you can often substitute one liqueur for another with a similar flavor profile. In general, whichever liqueur you choose will determine your drink's predominant flavor, or you can mix several together to create something complex. Here's what you need to know.

AMARI AND OTHER BITTER LIQUEURS

Amari refers to the large and varied group of Italian bitter liqueurs that are tailor-made for spritzing. Amaro (the singular form of amari) translates to "bitter" or "unsweetened," and though these concoctions are definitely sweetened, they are first and foremost bitter. That might not sound appealing, but when mixed with the fruitiness of sparkling wine and/or a splash of soda water and a handful of ice, these bracingly bitter liqueurs will recalibrate what your palate considers refreshing.

An amaro is traditionally made by infusing a neutral spirit base with a secret blend of bitter roots and herbs, as well as spices, fruits, and flowers, then aging it for a specific amount of time. Recipes are proprietary guarded secrets, and many brands have been in production for well over a hundred years, which is why they've built strong allegiances among different regions of Italy, and even among different generations. They're usually far lower in alcohol than regular spirits, but they can get up to 40 percent ABV.

Some amari are considered aperitivos, meant to be sipped before dinner to stimulate the appetite. Some are digestivos, meant to be sipped on their own after dinner to aid digestion, although it's just as traditional to mix them with soda water and sip them during the day. No matter what their original intention, these bitter liqueurs provide the necessary balance to create a bracingly refreshing spritz.

In addition to Italian amari, there's a huge world of French aperitifs, wine-based vermouths, and herbal liqueurs to play around with when looking for a spirited kick for your spritz.

VERMOUTHS

Vermouths aren't nearly as bitter as amari, but they are similarly infused with a bittering agent—wormwood, to be exact. They're wine based rather than spirits based, but are spiked with some high-proof alcohol. When it comes to using vermouths in spritzes, I think of them as amari-lite.

SPIRITS

Although classic spritzes are usually built with bittersweet (and low-proof) liqueurs, there's no reason you can't spike your drink with something stronger. Spirits not only add their own flavor dimension—brown sugar in the case of dark rum, botanicals in the case of gin—they also add a punch of boozy heat that can prop up a drink that tastes a bit weak. Have fun experimenting with your favorite styles and brands. Just keep in mind that a little goes a long way, and it can quickly overpower the mix if you pour with too heavy a hand.

An Aperitivo Awakening

Now that the world beyond Italy has embraced the bitter orange beauty of spritzy drinks featuring Campari and Aperol, lesser-known (and often more interesting) amari are getting wider distribution and finding a strong following among the new wave of aperitivo lovers.

Brands like Meletti 1870 Bitter, Casoni 1814 Aperitivo, Contratto Bitter, and Cappelletti Aperitivo Americano, with their orangey base and less aggressive bitterness, are giving Campari and Aperol a run for their money.

Then there's the growing appreciation for liqueurs with a more piney, herbaceous, alpine profile, like Braulio. Liqueurs made with naturally smoky Chinese rhubarb, a category called rabarbaro, are gaining steam, with Zucca being the most sweet and approachable and Cappelletti's Amaro Sfumato Rabarbaro more smoky and earthy.

Of course, that's just a drop in the amari bucket when it comes to European bitter liqueurs available in the United States. And now domestic producers are getting in on the action, with distillers and winemakers gaining a cult following for labels such as St. George Spirits' Bruto Americano and E & J Gallo's Lo-Fi aperitifs. These aperitivo-style liqueurs are interesting, complex, and bracingly bitter, but a big part of the growing appeal is the low ABV—generally around 16 to 20 percent, which is just a bit higher than the typical glass of wine, far lower than spirits, and greatly reduced when the liqueur is mixed with things like tonic, soda water, and juice.

A natural progression of this better-for-you cocktail category is the recent explosion of nonalcoholic spirits, like Seedlip and Ritual, and aperitif look-alikes, such as Lyre's and Ghia. Offering complex flavors and bitterness with zero ABV, they make the aperitivo lifestyle attainable anytime and for everyone.

Sparkling Wine

Almost every boozy spritz in this book has some sort of sparkling wine, whether that's prosecco, Cava, Champagne, or a bubbly rosé or fruity Lambrusco. It's just one of the essential ways a cocktail is identified as a spritz, not a highball (spirit and soda on ice) or a fizz (spirit and soda straight). After all, the sparkling wine accounts for most of the volume in a spritz, and there's no "right" way to make such a relaxed and easy-going drink. There's only what's right for you. You want a sweeter drink? Go with a sweeter style of sparkling wine. Want to enhance the bitter, palate-piquing edge? Go with a brut. Another great thing about brut wines in spritzes is that you'll be better able to control the sweetness of your drink. Many amari, though bitter, are also very sweet. By opting for a low-residual-sugar wine, you don't run the risk of creating a too-sweet drink, and you can always sweeten it to taste with simple syrup (see page 28). There are a couple of combinations that work better with just soda water, spicy ginger beer, or a form of tonic water providing the effervescence, but mostly you're going to need to stock up on some bubbly wine.

Soda Water

Also known as seltzer, sparkling water, and club soda, soda water lightens up a spritz. It makes for a more refreshing drink and keeps the ABV low to boot. But don't use too much or the drink will taste watered down. Any fizzy water works. The bubblier, the better. If you have a SodaStream that you can pump with maximum CO_2, you're ahead of the game. Barring that, get the bubbliest carbonated water you can. Fever-Tree, Topo Chico, Schweppes, and Canada Dry all make aggressively fizzy soda water ideal for spritzing. And when extra flavor is necessary, there's a whole world of flavored fizzy water at your disposal. Coconut, in particular, is excellent in a spritz.

Mix-Ins

Juices and syrups, ginger beer and pale ale—all of these and more have found their way into the recipes in this book. Although traditional spritzes are made with just three ingredients, stirring in one of these flavor-packed additions can transform the drink into something unique. Two things to keep in mind are the viscosity and the sweetness level. The mix-ins used here generally steer clear of anything too thick and opaque, like dairy products or purees, because they weigh down the bubbles and get in the way of refreshment. And the juices, tonics, sodas, and mixers are the lowest level of sweetness whenever possible. That's because the liqueurs and sparkling wine bring their own sugars to the party, and you don't want to end up with liquid dessert. You can always sweeten to taste.

See pages 152-166 for recommendations on specific liqueurs, sparkling wines, and other spritz-worthy additions.

TOOLS

Technically, you don't need a single tool to make a standard spritz—especially once you have some experience under your belt. Using three parts liqueur, two parts sparkling wine, and a splash of sparkling water to taste, you could totally skip the jigger and just eyeball your pours. But when you want to venture into more complex territory, or even just achieve some consistency among drinks, a few common kitchen gadgets will help you get there. Here are the tools you'll need.

Blender, Immersion Blender, or Juicer

Ideal for extracting the juice from non-citrus fruits, like melons and pineapple. If you don't have a juicer, you can puree the fruit in a blender or an immersion blender, then strain out the solids.

Champagne Stopper

Spritzes don't use that much sparkling wine, so chances are you're going to end up with a half-full bottle most of the time. Seal it off with a stopper and it'll stay fizzy in the fridge for days. Simple and inexpensive stoppers work great in my experience. They're like a mechanical cork: Stick it in the opening of the bottle, then press the lever to lock it in place.

Citrus Reamer

Absolutely essential for squeezing every last bit of juice from lemons, limes, oranges, and grapefruits.

Cocktail Picks

For charming skewered garnishes, you'll need 4- to 6-inch-long (10 to 15 cm) wood or bamboo sandwich or cocktail picks (see Resources, page 172). Regular toothpicks aren't long enough to properly skewer enough ingredients to make a garnish for a big spritz-filled wineglass.

Fine-Mesh Sieves (Large and Small)

Use a large sieve to strain the juice from pureed fruits. Use a small sieve to strain muddled mixtures over ice, or to strain seeds and pulp from citrus juice.

Glassware

Venetian spritz tradition calls for a large wineglass, but really any generously sized glass with a wide rim will serve the purpose. A large rocks glass works great—anything called a double rocks glass, a double old-fashioned glass, or a tumbler. Even a tall highball glass or plain drinking glass will suffice. The goal is to choose a glass with enough room for a generous handful of ice and about 6 ounces (175 ml) of liquid to swirl around, and ideally enough height to give the bubbles a runway. A narrow opening may preserve some of the bubbles, but a wider opening accommodates garnishes better, is easier to sip from without a straw, and allows you to enjoy more of the aroma. It's up to you. But save your flutes, martini glasses, and antique coupes for another drink.

Grater (Microplane)

For grating fresh ginger or zesting citrus.

Measuring Spoons

Ideal for measuring out ingredients used in small amounts, like rose water, turmeric, and grated ginger.

Mini Measuring Beaker Set or Jigger

Although you can just eyeball a classic three-ingredient spritz, if you want to make things a tad bit easier, get the OXO Good Grips mini measuring cup or OXO mini beaker set (see Resources, page 172). They measure from 1/4 ounce (7 ml) up to 2 ounces (60 ml), so it's easy to precisely measure and dial in flavors just right. Or go old-school and opt for a set of jiggers. You'll want one that has 1- and 2-ounce (30 and 60 ml) measures, and one with 1/2- and 3/4-ounce (15 and 20 ml) measures.

Mixing Glass and/or Cocktail Shaker

Muddling ingredients (i.e., pounding them with a stick in a glass) is a lot safer in a heavy-bottomed mixing glass. The tin of a cocktail shaker will work too, and a shaker is the best way to break up and liquefy jam, such as in the Figgy Pudding spritz on page 143.

Muddler

This is a wood or plastic stick (sometimes with spikes on the bottom) used right in the glass to bruise herbs to release their essential oils, or to puree small amounts of fruit.

Paring Knife

For cutting fruit and removing citrus peels for garnish.

Vegetable Peeler

A Y-shaped peeler works best for peeling large swaths of citrus peel, or even cucumber, for garnishes. However, a regular straight peeler works fine too.

HOW TO ACHIEVE
SPRITZ PERFECTION

Spritzes are laid-back by nature, so it seems almost silly to start micro-managing their construction. And the recipes in this book, like those for all spritzes, are ideal for riffing. If you want to use a little more of this and a little less of that, by all means do it. Still, if you want a good, refreshing drink, not lukewarm plonk, you do need to consider a few things—namely, how to make your spritz absolutely cold.

1. Chill the wine (at least). A spritz is, after all, almost completely made of sparkling wine and a splash of soda—4 to 6 ounces' (120 to 175 ml) worth. If you rely only on the ice to chill the liquids, you will quickly end up with a big glass of tepid, watered-down booze—the absolute opposite of refreshment. If you don't have room in your fridge to keep a bottle of prosecco cold, try canned sparkling wine (both white and rosé). It would be ideal if you could make room for your most-used amari and vermouths too.

2. Chill the glass (if you can remember). This is especially important in the heat of summer, when we all want to be sipping our spritzes poolside (or at least sprinkler-side). A cold glass will keep the drink colder longer. Try to keep a few wineglasses in your freezer, or tuck them in about 30 minutes before spritz time. No freezer room? Fill the glasses with ice and cold water and let them hang out until frosty, then dump the contents and proceed with mixing your drink.

3. Use fresh ice (always). Spritzes require a lot of ice, since you want the glass about three-quarters full. Therefore, the quality of your ice matters (see page 163). Use fresh ice cubes made from good-tasting water.

HOW TO BUILD A SPRITZ

Usually just three ingredients mixed right in the glass, a spritz cocktail is the very definition of simplicity. Still, there are a few things you should do if you want to attain spritz perfection.

Add a big handful of ice cubes to a generously sized glass. Don't use crushed ice, which will dilute the drink too quickly.

Pour the amaro over the ice. Add sparkling wine and soda water last to preserve their fizz. (The water will dilute and lighten the drink, so adjust to taste.)

Raise a spoon or straw up and down a few times to move the ice and gently blend the ingredients without flattening the bubbles.

Garnish and serve.

FROM LEFT TO RIGHT: Mint Simple Syrup, Peach-Lavender Shrub, Honey Simple Syrup, Strawberry-Rhubarb Syrup, Lavender Simple Syrup, Strawberry-Rose Shrub, Vanilla Simple Syrup, Raspberry-Thyme Shrub (see Syrups and Shrubs, pages 28-34).

SYRUPS AND SHRUBS

Sometimes it takes a little heat and a little time to get fruits and herbs spritz-ready. That's where these easy-to-make tart and sweet syrups and juicy shrubs come in. They add tons of flavor to a wide range of drinks.

SIMPLE SYRUP

With this basic recipe, which you can scale up or down as you need, you can make a versatile syrup to sweeten any drink, or a huge array of flavored syrups. For the variations, follow this basic recipe, and add the herbs or other ingredients along with the sugar and water. For a stronger flavor, let the herbs steep in the mixture overnight in the fridge before straining. Each simple syrup will keep for about a month in an airtight container in the fridge.

MAKES 1¼ CUPS (300 ML)

1 cup (240 ml) water

1 cup (200 g) sugar

In a small saucepan, combine the water and sugar and set the pan over medium-low heat, stirring until the sugar dissolves. (Or in a small microwave-safe bowl, microwave the water and sugar for about 1 minute, then stir until the sugar dissolves into the water.) Allow the mixture to cool, transfer the syrup to an airtight container, and refrigerate.

Basil Simple Syrup

Add 1 cup (30 g) packed fresh basil leaves to the water and sugar mixture before heating. Bring to a simmer, allow the mixture to cool, strain out the herbs, transfer the syrup to an airtight container, and refrigerate.

Lavender Simple Syrup

Add 2 tablespoons dried lavender buds (see Resources, page 172) to the water and sugar mixture before heating. Bring to a simmer, allow the mixture to cool, strain out the herbs, transfer the syrup to an airtight container, and refrigerate.

Mint Simple Syrup

Add ¾ cup (25 g) packed fresh mint leaves to the water and sugar mixture before heating. Bring to a simmer, allow the mixture to cool, strain out the herbs, transfer the syrup to an airtight container, and refrigerate.

Rosemary Simple Syrup

Add 3 large (about 4-inch-long/10 cm) fresh rosemary sprigs to the water and sugar mixture before heating. Bring to a simmer, allow the mixture to cool, strain out the herbs, transfer the syrup to an airtight container, and refrigerate.

Thyme Simple Syrup

Add ½ cup (5 g) fresh thyme sprigs to the water and sugar mixture before heating. Bring to a simmer, allow the mixture to cool, strain out the herbs, transfer the syrup to an airtight container, and refrigerate.

Vanilla Simple Syrup

Add 1 vanilla bean, split in half lengthwise and seeds scraped into the pan with the water and sugar, along with the pod. After heating, allow the mixture to cool, remove the pod, transfer the syrup to an airtight container, and refrigerate. (The pod still has tons of flavor; rinse, dry, and place it in a container of sugar for vanilla-scented sugar or add it to a bottle of vanilla extract.)

HONEY SIMPLE SYRUP

When you use honey simple syrup, you really want to taste the honey, so I don't like to dilute it too much. It's more a matter of adding enough water to liquefy the honey, and keeping it that way, so it mixes into drinks better. But if you want this syrup less sweet, just add an equal amount of water.

MAKES ¾ CUP (180 ML)

½ cup (170 g) honey

¼ cup (60 ml) water

In a small saucepan, combine the honey and water, set the pan over low heat, and stir until the honey is dissolved. (Or in a microwave-safe bowl, microwave the honey and water for about 30 seconds, then stir until the honey melts and dissolves into the water.) Allow to cool, transfer to an airtight container, and refrigerate. The syrup will keep for about a month.

STRAWBERRY-RHUBARB SYRUP

Strawberries by themselves can be almost too demure and sweet, while on its own, rhubarb is vegetal and stringently tart. When combined, each makes the other better, filling in where the other leaves off. No wonder you'll want to drizzle this syrup into everything. Depending on the season and varietal, some berries are sweeter than others. Start with the lesser amount of sugar, then taste the syrup and add more if it needs more sweetness.

MAKES ABOUT 2 CUPS (480 ML)

1 pound (455 g) fresh or frozen strawberries, hulled

8 ounces (225 g) fresh or frozen rhubarb, chopped

1 cup (240 ml) water

1/2 cup (100 g) sugar, plus more (optional) to taste

In a large saucepan, combine the strawberries, rhubarb, water, and 1/2 cup (100 g) sugar. Cover and bring to a simmer over medium heat, stirring occasionally, until the fruit is very tender, about 10 minutes. Allow to cool, then strain into a bowl through a fine-mesh sieve, pressing on the solids to extract the liquid (you can save the fruit to add to a smoothie or spoon on top of yogurt). Taste and add more sugar, if desired. Transfer the syrup to an airtight container and refrigerate. The syrup will keep for 1 week.

PEACH-LAVENDER SHRUB

Lavender always blooms right around the same time that peaches are ready for picking—just one more reason why they're a perfect farm pairing. What grows together, goes together.

MAKES ABOUT 2 CUPS (480 ML)

1 pound (455 g) fresh, ripe peaches (about 4 peaches), pitted and chopped (no need to peel)

1 tablespoon dried lavender buds (see Resources, page 172)

1 cup (200 g) sugar

1 cup (240 ml) apple cider vinegar

In a medium bowl, stir and gently mash the peaches and lavender with the sugar until the fruit is fully coated. Cover and refrigerate overnight or for up to 2 days. Strain the mixture into a nonreactive bowl through a fine-mesh sieve, pressing on the solids to extract the liquid; discard the fruit solids. Stir in the vinegar. Cover and refrigerate for 5 days to allow the vinegar to mellow before using. The shrub will keep for 1 month.

STRAWBERRY-ROSE SHRUB

This is such a gorgeously hued, deliciously fragrant shrub, you won't be able to resist sipping it straight or with just a bit of soda water. Look for dried rose petals at tea and spice shops.

MAKES ABOUT 2 CUPS (480 ML)

1 pound (455 g) fresh or frozen strawberries, hulled

2 tablespoons dried rose petals (see Resources, page 172)

1 cup (200 g) sugar

1 cup (240 ml) apple cider vinegar

In a medium bowl, stir and gently mash the strawberries and rose petals with the sugar until the fruit is fully coated. Cover and refrigerate overnight or for up to 2 days. Strain the mixture into a nonreactive bowl through a fine-mesh sieve, pressing on the solids to extract the liquid; discard the fruit solids. Stir in the vinegar. Cover and refrigerate for 5 days to allow the vinegar to mellow before using. The shrub will keep for 1 month.

RASPBERRY-THYME SHRUB

Combining herbs with raspberries adds an element of freshness to the berries' rich, jammy flavor. Rosemary, mint, and lemon verbena are all great options if you want to try something other than the thyme used here.

MAKES ABOUT 1 CUP (240 ML)

8 ounces (225 g) fresh or frozen raspberries

1 tablespoon fresh thyme leaves

¼ cup (50 g) sugar

½ cup (120 ml) apple cider vinegar

In a medium bowl, stir and gently mash the raspberries and thyme leaves with the sugar until the fruit and herbs are fully coated. Cover and refrigerate overnight or for up to 2 days. Strain the mixture into a nonreactive bowl through a fine-mesh sieve, pressing on the solids to extract the liquid; discard the fruit solids. Stir in the vinegar. Cover and refrigerate for 5 days to allow the vinegar to mellow before using. The shrub will keep for 1 month.

GARNISHES

As free-spirited as spritzes can be, you should still take the time to add a garnish. It doesn't have to be fancy. It can be as simple as a slice of citrus floating along the side of the glass, but even that is an important finishing touch. If you think about it, most cocktails come with a garnish of some sort, and that's because garnishes often add an important aromatic and flavor component to a drink. And, of course, they make it far more visually appealing too. Here are some of the most common garnishes that add panache to a spritz.

Citrus Peels

Run a vegetable peeler (preferably Y-shaped) over the citrus from top to bottom in one smooth, firm stroke, getting some (but not much) white pith. Squeeze the peel over the drink, either by twisting or folding in half, to express the oils over the surface. Drop it in, colorful-side up.

Fans

For firm, round fruits, like apples and Asian pears, stand the fruit on a cutting board and slice off one side of it, next to the core. Place the fruit cut-side down (the stem and bottom ends should be to your left and right, perpendicular to the bottom edge of the cutting board) and thinly slice. This will create pointed instead of round tips. Fan out the pieces and skewer to keep in place. For strawberries, set hull-side

down and thinly slice from top to bottom, not cutting through the hull, which will hold the slices in place. Fan out and settle onto the drink.

Herbs and Flowers

Choose fresh, upright, long herb sprigs (flowering herbs can be a nice touch) or edible flowers (roses, orchids, pansies, nasturtiums, borage, and chamomile, to name a few) and tuck into the glass so they stand 2 inches (5 cm) above the rim. Mint can be bundled into a generous bouquet. Try using a combination of herbs and flowers.

Pineapple Triangles and Leaves

For triangles, keep the peel on for maximum visual impact, or remove if you like. Cut the top and bottom off the pineapple, cut crosswise into ¾-inch (2 cm) circles, then cut the circles into eighths. Cut a slit in the pointy end and set on the rim of the glass, or cut the slit on the long side of the triangle and set on the rim at that angle. For pineapple leaves, choose the best-looking ones and trim with

scissors to neaten the edges if necessary. You can use pinking shears for a zigzag edge. Tuck into the glass so at least 2 inches (5 cm) rise above the rim.

Ribbons

Run a vegetable peeler down the length of a cucumber or spiral around the circumference of a citrus or apple (ends trimmed flat first) to remove a long continuous piece of flexible peel. If the edges are rough, feel free to trim them straight. Cucumber ribbons can be made of the peel for a dark green garnish, or of the flesh for a light green garnish. Spiral the peel along the inside of the glass, adding ice as you go to anchor it in place, or use chopsticks to fit it into place after the drink is made.

Skewers

Use a 4- to 6-inch (10 to 15 cm) wooden sandwich pick or bamboo cocktail pick to skewer two or more garnishes together, from the traditional olives or cherries to chunks of pineapple or peach. Get creative: You can combine olives or fruit with herbs, thread cucumber ribbons or pineapple leaves, or skewer a triangular slice of citrus peel to make a mini sail.

Wedges

Choose juicy fruits. For lemons and limes, trim just a bit off the top and bottom to round any points. Cut into quarters lengthwise. If the wedges are really thick, cut them in half lengthwise again. You can squeeze the wedge over the drink and drop it in or cut a slit crosswise through the flesh and set it onto the rim of the glass. You can also cut stone fruits into wedges, though their

delicate flesh means they're best dropped in the glass. Melon scooped into balls with a melon baller tool is a fun garnish too.

Wheels and Half-Wheels (and a Twist)

Cut whole citrus crosswise for a full wheel, or cut in half first to create half-wheels. Pick out any seeds. Tuck the wheel or half-wheel between the ice and the side of the glass so it's visible. To create a twist to float on top, cut the flesh of the wheel straight down from the center to the edge, twist the two sides away from each other, and set on top of the drink.

Before you venture into the world of modern spritzes, it helps to know what came before. Get acquainted with these icons and you'll have a better frame of reference for riffing.

APEROL SPRITZ
(AKA VENETIAN SPRITZ)

Liquid summer

Hailing from Venice, where the Aperol amaro is king, this sunny, citrusy, bitter-sweet spritz is responsible for kicking off a worldwide renaissance. If you swap out the Aperol for its more bitter cousin, Campari, or the lusher, vanilla-scented Cappelletti Aperitivo Americano (or even a combination), simply call this by its original name: Venetian Spritz.

MAKES 1

2 ounces (60 ml) Aperol
(or similar bitter orange amaro;
see Resources, page 170)

3 ounces (90 ml) prosecco, chilled

2 ounces (60 ml) soda water, chilled

Orange half-wheel, for garnish
(see page 37)

Skewered green olives, for garnish
(optional; see page 37)

Fill a wineglass three-quarters full with ice. Pour the Aperol and prosecco over the ice and top with the soda water. Gently stir to combine. Tuck the orange half-wheel between the ice and the side of the glass and add the skewered olives, if using.

VARIATION

For a zero-proof drink, fill a wineglass three-quarters full with ice. Pour 2 ounces (60 ml) Crodino (see Resources, page 169), 2 ounces (60 ml) Sanpellegrino Aranciata or Aranciata Rossa orange soda (see Resources, page 170), and 1 to 2 ounces (30 to 60 ml) soda water over the ice. Gently stir to combine and garnish as directed.

WHITE WINE SPRITZER

The spandex-era throwback gets an upgrade.

Although the name conjures up images of feathered hair and fern bars from back when white wine spritzers were the low-cal drink of choice among ladies in the diet-crazed '80s, it's actually the drink that birthed the category. White wine with a "spritz" of water was how Austrian soldiers stationed in northern Italy in the 1800s could tolerate the local vino (which was not to their Riesling-attuned taste). The key to making this a great drink is using a very aromatic wine and adding an intriguing dash of bitters. Garnish with the citrus that goes best with the wine you choose; a few wedges of fresh stone fruit or berries wouldn't be amiss either.

MAKES 1

6 ounces (175 ml) aromatic white wine (such as Riesling or Gewürztraminer), chilled

2 ounces (60 ml) soda water, chilled

Dash of orange, grapefruit, or Angostura bitters (see Resources, page 169)

Lime, lemon, or orange peel, for garnish (see page 35)

Fill a wineglass three-quarters full with ice. Pour the wine over the ice, then top with the soda water. Gently stir to combine. Add the bitters. Twist the citrus peel over the drink, and drop it in to garnish.

VARIATION

For a more floral cocktail, use an aromatic but dry white wine, like Sauvignon Blanc, Albariño, or Torrontés, and add 1 ounce (30 ml) St-Germain elderflower liqueur (see Resources, page 171).

NEGRONI SBAGLIATO

Bitter orange meets sparkling wine.

Some consider this a spritzified Negroni without the gin, but it's really like an Americano (see page 48) with prosecco instead of soda water, making this 1970s creation a bit boozier and a bit sweeter thanks to the wine. As with the Americano, you can stray from tradition and swap in Dolin Blanc dry vermouth instead of sweet. *Sbagliato* means "incorrect" or "mistake" in Italian, which would be accurate if you're a Negroni purist, but if you ask me, the drink is a stroke of genius.

MAKES 1

1½ ounces (45 ml) Campari
(see Resources, page 170)

1½ ounces (45 ml) sweet vermouth, such as Carpano Antica Formula, or dry vermouth, such as Dolin Blanc (see Resources, page 171)

3 ounces (90 ml) prosecco, chilled

Orange half-wheel, for garnish
(see page 37)

Fill a wineglass three-quarters full with ice. Pour the Campari, vermouth, and prosecco over the ice. Gently stir to combine. Tuck the orange half-wheel between the ice and the side of the glass.

BICICLETTA

No prosecco? No problem.

This bracing drink is said to be named for the bicycles old Italian gents would wobble home on following an afternoon of drinking with friends. Or maybe it's because mixing one up is as effortless as riding a bike. It's simply dry white wine livened up with bitter orange Campari and a splash of soda water. Make this sipper when you're out of bubbly but have a good bottle of pinot grigio on hand.

MAKES 1

2 ounces (60 ml) Campari
(see Resources, page 170)

2 ounces (60 ml) dry Italian white wine, such as pinot grigio, chilled

1 to 2 ounces (30 to 60 ml) soda water, chilled

Orange or lemon wheel, for garnish (see page 37)

Fill a wineglass three-quarters full with ice. Pour the Campari and wine over the ice, then top with the soda water. Gently stir to combine. Tuck the orange or lemon wheel between the ice and the side of the glass.

THE HUGO

Like minty, floral limeade

This youngster in the spritz canon is ideal for those who crave the flavor of juicy lime, with mint and elderflower adding sweet and breezy refreshment. A lime-juice-enhanced riff on the original created in 2005 by bartender Roland "AK" Gruber in the South Tyrol region of Italy, it took off like wildfire, and with good reason.

MAKES 1

2 mint sprigs

2 ounces (60 ml) St-Germain elderflower liqueur (see Resources, page 171)

¼ ounce (7 ml) fresh lime juice

3 ounces (90 ml) prosecco, chilled

1 ounce (30 ml) elderflower tonic water (preferably Q Mixers; see Resources, page 170), plain tonic water, or soda water, chilled

2 lime wheels, for garnish (see page 37)

Muddle the leaves from 1 mint sprig in a sturdy wineglass. Fill the glass three-quarters full with ice and pour the St-Germain, lime juice, and prosecco over the ice. Top with the elderflower tonic. Gently stir to combine. Garnish with the remaining mint sprig and tuck the lime wheels between the ice and the side of the glass.

VARIATION

For a zero-proof drink, muddle the leaves from 1 mint sprig in a sturdy wineglass. Fill the glass three-quarters full with ice. Pour 1½ ounces (45 ml) elderflower syrup (such as IKEA or D'Arbo brands; see Resources, page 172), ½ ounce (15 ml) fresh lime juice, 2 ounces (60 ml) soda water, and 2 ounces (60 ml) elderflower tonic water over the ice. Gently stir to combine and garnish as directed.

AMERICANO

Campari + soda = citrusy bittersweet refreshment

There's no sparkling wine in this proto-Negroni from the 1920s, but the Americano is bracingly bitter, bubbly, and low alcohol, which fits the spritz profile perfectly. It's a classic riff on the Milano-Torino cocktail, a simple mix of Campari (from Milan) and sweet vermouth (from Turin) created by Gaspare Campari at his Caffè Campari in the 1860s. As one story goes, when soda water was added, it became a refreshing hit among American tourists, hence the name. Although sweet vermouth is traditional, a lighter dry vermouth (such as Dolin Blanc) lets the Campari flavor and color shine through. For a boozier cocktail, add 1 ounce (30 ml) gin.

MAKES 1

1½ ounces (45 ml) Campari
(see Resources, page 170)

1½ ounces (45 ml) sweet vermouth, such as Carpano Antica Formula, or dry vermouth, such as Dolin Blanc (see Resources, page 171)

3 ounces (90 ml) soda water, chilled

Orange half-wheel, for garnish
(see page 37)

Fill a wineglass three-quarters full with ice. Pour the Campari, vermouth, and soda water over the ice. Gently stir to combine. Tuck the orange half-wheel between the ice and the side of the glass or set it on top.

AMERICAN MULE

Give your ginger beer a kick.

Technically, a mule is not a spritz, but with just a smidge of spirits and plenty of bubbles, it's certainly spritz-like. This rye whiskey version, with its woodsy spice notes complementing the zesty ginger beer, is far more interesting than the original vodka-based Moscow Mule, but of course the choice is up to you. To keep the sweetness in check, opt for a not-too-sweet ginger beer.

MAKES 1

1 ounce (30 ml) rye whiskey, such as Bulleit (see Resources, page 170)

3 ounces (90 ml) ginger beer, preferably Q Mixers (see Resources, page 170), chilled

2 lime wedges, 1 for garnish (see page 37)

Mint sprig and/or candied ginger, for garnish (see page 36)

Fill a wineglass or mule mug three-quarters full with ice. Pour the whiskey and ginger beer over the ice. Squeeze 1 lime wedge into the drink and discard. Gently stir to combine. Cut a slit in the remaining lime wedge and set on the rim of the glass. Tuck the mint sprig and/or candied ginger between the ice and the side of the glass.

HOLD THE
BOOZE

TONIC AND BITTERS

Keeping it classic

The T&B is the original spritz-like mocktail: just tonic water (or soda water, if you prefer) over ice, with a generous addition of (usually) Angostura bitters and a squeeze of lemon or lime. It's the ideal drink to order at any bar when you want to go light on the booze. This version is a more floral and citrusy take on the classic and an open invitation to experiment with your own favorite bitters. Keep in mind that bitters do contain alcohol, though they're used in such small amounts they won't make you tipsy. Still, if you want to keep your drink completely free of spirits, you might want to skip this one.

MAKES 1

6 ounces (175 ml) elderflower tonic water, preferably Q Mixers (see Resources, page 170), chilled

½ to 1 teaspoon grapefruit bitters (see Resources, page 169)

1 lemon wedge, for garnish (see page 37)

Fill a wineglass three-quarters full with ice. Pour the elderflower tonic over the ice. Add the grapefruit bitters. Gently stir to combine. Squeeze the lemon wedge into the drink and drop it in.

Spritz-Worthy Snacks

In Italy, a spritz is almost always served with a few snacks, a little something to whet the appetite. Green olives and potato chips are the old-school ubiquitous duo, but different regions add their own spin too. In Veneto, the cicchetti, as these snacks are called, traditionally include seafood, like marinated sardines and grilled pulpo (octopus), but have evolved to include nearly any kind of bite-size snack. Think polpette (meatballs) or tramezzini, which are basically Italian-style tea sandwiches of crustless white bread spread with a generous layer of good butter or mayo and topped with things like tuna and olives, cured meats, or grilled vegetables and cheese. The sandwiches are then cut into small triangles or squares (in which case they're called francobolli, or postage stamps). Other regions serve these too, often in full-on buffets that sport everything from pizza to polenta.

Here are some ideas for your own aperitivo hour.

- Marinated olives
- Salty potato chips
- Marcona almonds
- Slices of prosciutto, mortadella, or other salumi
- Antipasto skewers of small fresh mozzarella balls, sliced cured meats, fresh basil leaves, marinated or pickled peppers, artichoke hearts, and/or olives
- Slices of salty cheese like Pecorino Romano or Parmigiano-Reggiano
- Taralli, breadsticks, or crackers
- Focaccia or pizza
- Tramezzini featuring asparagus and hard-cooked eggs, tuna and tapenade, bresaola and arugula, or shrimp salad
- A baguette or rolls filled with salumi, cheese, and/ or antipasto vegetables

CONTINUED

- Crostini or grilled polenta squares topped with baccalà mantecato (salt cod puree), 'nduja (fermented spreadable salumi) and arugula, lardo (thinly shaved cured pork fat) and radicchio, diced tomatoes and caponata (a sweet-sour eggplant relish), or chicken liver pâté and pickled onions

- Bruschetta with marinated tomatoes or pesto and grilled vegetables or seafood

- Fritters such as arancini (fried risotto balls), supplì (arancini stuffed with mozzarella), baccalà, or zucchini or other vegetables

- Frittata squares

- Polpette

- Prosciutto-wrapped melon slices

- Cut vegetables and artichoke-Parmesan dip

- Fried ravioli with marinara sauce

- Small plates of pasta

- Endive leaves filled with Gorgonzola, diced celery and apple, and toasted walnuts

- Radishes, cultured butter, and sea salt

- Savory vegetable tarts

- Pickled green beans or peppers

- Stuffed fried zucchini blossoms

- Fritto misto (battered and fried vegetables)

- Fricos (grated Parmesan crisps)

- Panelle (Sicilian chickpea "fries")

Honeyed floral flavors and beguiling herbal elixirs transform into light and fizzy ambrosia when given the spritz treatment. They're ideal for spring soirées and breezy summer afternoons.

FRENCH SPRITZ

Think elderflower lemonade for grown-ups.

The world is drenched in spritzes made with quintessentially French ingredients like Champagne and St-Germain. This spritz is no different. It's based on the iconic French 75 (a lightly sweetened mix of gin, lemon juice, and Champagne), but instead of sugar it uses St-Germain for a more floral touch. The gin is kept to a minimum, offering just the right amount of structure while keeping the ABV low. Instead of London dry style, go for one of the more intriguingly botanical New Western gins turning heads these days (see page 161); French-made G'Vine (see Resources, page 171) would be a great choice.

MAKES 1

2 ounces (60 ml) St-Germain elderflower liqueur (see Resources, page 171)

1/2 ounce (15 ml) fresh lemon juice

1/4 ounce (7 ml) gin (floral and French, if you have it)

3 ounces (90 ml) Champagne (or other sparkling wine), chilled

2 ounces (60 ml) soda water, chilled

Lemon peel, for garnish (see page 35)

Blossoming herb sprig such as thyme, for garnish (see page 36)

Fill a wineglass three-quarters full with ice. Pour the St-Germain, lemon juice, gin, and Champagne over the ice. Top with the soda water. Gently stir to combine. Twist the lemon peel over the glass and drop it in. Garnish with the herb sprig.

VARIATION

For a zero-proof drink, fill a wineglass three-quarters full with ice. Pour 1 1/2 ounces (45 ml) elderflower syrup (such as IKEA or D'Arbo brands; see Resources, page 172), 3/4 ounce (20 ml) fresh lemon juice, 1/4 to 1/2 ounce (7 to 15 ml) Seedlip Garden 108 (see Resources, page 171), 2 to 3 ounces (60 to 90 ml) soda water, and 2 ounces (60 ml) tonic water over the ice. Gently stir to combine and garnish as directed.

LADY LAVENDER

Blackberry-licious

Fresh blackberries, aromatic gin, and lavender simple syrup combine to make a fruity-floral, scarlet-purple, garden-fresh sipper. You can strain out the berry solids for a cleaner-looking drink as instructed here, or leave them in for even more vibrant color. They sink to the bottom of the glass and create a dramatic fade from dark purple to light.

MAKES 1

¼ cup (about 1¼ ounces/35 g) fresh blackberries (about 5 berries)

1 ounce (30 ml) gin, preferably New Western style, such as Thinking Tree (see Resources, page 172) or another floral gin

1 ounce (30 ml) Lavender Simple Syrup (page 29)

1 ounce (30 ml) fresh lemon juice

2 ounces (60 ml) prosecco, chilled

2 ounces (60 ml) lavender Dry Botanical Bubbly (see Resources, page 169) or plain soda water, chilled

Skewered blackberries, for garnish (optional; see page 37)

Lavender sprig, for garnish (see page 36)

In a mixing glass or cocktail shaker, muddle the blackberries with the gin, simple syrup, and lemon juice. Fill a wineglass three-quarters full with ice. Strain the blackberry mixture over the ice, pressing on the solids to extract the liquid. Add the prosecco and top with the lavender soda. Gently stir to combine. Add the skewered blackberries, if using, and lavender sprig.

VARIATION

For a zero-proof drink, omit the gin and replace the prosecco with 2 ounces (60 ml) more lavender Dry Botanical Bubbly or elderflower tonic water (preferably Q Mixers; see Resources, page 170).

RESPECT YOUR ELDERS

A botanical beauty

This sunny yellow sipper is comfortingly floral but with an herbal edge, and lemony but with a pithy bitterness. That's because it has a healthy pour of Suze, an esoterically complex and perfumed favorite aperitif of the French—and the spirit equivalent of an elegant older Parisian who doesn't suffer fools. A little elderflower liqueur enhances its floral aromas while taming that bitter bite.

MAKES 1

1 ounce (30 ml) St-Germain
elderflower liqueur
(see Resources, page 171)

3/4 ounce (20 ml) Suze aperitif
(see Resources, page 170)

3 ounces (90 ml) prosecco, chilled

1 lemon wedge

1 ounce (30 ml) elderflower tonic
water (preferably Q Mixers;
see Resources, page 170), or
plain tonic water, chilled

Mint sprig, for garnish (see page 36)

Fill a wineglass three-quarters full with ice. Pour the St-Germain, Suze, and prosecco over the ice. Squeeze the lemon wedge into the drink and drop it in. Top with the tonic water. Gently stir to combine. Garnish with the mint sprig.

THE ROSÉ GARDEN

Strawberries, roses, and a splash of orange

The flavor of rose seems to enhance all that is sweet and beautiful about strawberries. For this drink, you can turn dried rose petals and intensely sweet strawberries into a luscious yet piquant shrub that adds a burst of fruity, floral juiciness to sparkling rosé. To give it just a smidge of mouthwatering bitterness, include a splash of Cappelletti too; since it's sweet and relatively mild with tons of vanilla, the citrusy amaro provides a pleasant backdrop rather than taking center stage.

MAKES 1

1 ounce (30 ml) Strawberry-Rose Shrub (page 33)

¾ ounce (20 ml) Cappelletti Aperitivo Americano (see Resources, page 170)

2 ounces (60 ml) sparkling rosé, chilled

2 ounces (60 ml) soda water, chilled

1 lime wedge, for garnish (see page 37)

Skewered strawberries, for garnish (see page 37)

Fill a wineglass three-quarters full with ice. Pour the shrub and Cappelletti over the ice. Add the sparkling rosé and top with the soda water. Gently stir to combine. Squeeze the lime wedge into the drink and drop it in. Garnish with the skewered strawberries.

VARIATION

For a zero-proof drink, fill a wineglass three-quarters full with ice. Pour 1½ ounces (45 ml) soda water, 1½ ounces (45 ml) strawberry-rose shrub, and 3 ounces (90 ml) vanilla Dry Botanical Bubbly (see Resources, page 169) over the ice. Gently stir to combine and garnish as directed.

SUN DAY

Peaches drizzled in lavender honey—but in liquid form

Light gold, like the sun shining through the trees on a late August afternoon, this lavender-peach spritz combines two iconic summertime flavors. The sweet peach and honeyed Lillet balance the pronounced lavender notes in the simple syrup, resulting in a refreshingly juicy drink that's softly perfumed.

MAKES 1

2 ounces (60 ml) Lillet Blanc aperitif (see Resources, page 171)

1 ounce (30 ml) Peach-Lavender Shrub (page 32)

½ ounce (15 ml) Lavender Simple Syrup (page 29)

2 ounces (60 ml) prosecco, chilled

1 ounce (30 ml) elderflower tonic water, preferably Q Mixers (see Resources, page 170), chilled

Peach wedge, for garnish (see page 37)

Lavender sprig, for garnish (see page 36)

Fill a wineglass three-quarters full with ice. Pour the Lillet, shrub, and simple syrup over the ice. Add the prosecco and top with the elderflower tonic. Gently stir to combine. Cut a slit in the peach wedge and set on the rim of the glass or tuck it between the ice and the glass and add the lavender sprig.

VARIATION

For a zero-proof drink, fill a wineglass three-quarters full with ice. Pour 4 ounces (120 ml) elderflower tonic water, ½ ounce (15 ml) lavender simple syrup, and 2 ounces (60 ml) peach-lavender shrub over the ice. Gently stir to combine and garnish as directed.

THE CHANTEUSE

Beguilingly botanical

An aura of mystery surrounds this drink because it tastes like there's gin, but there isn't a drop of it, and there's a hefty dose of grapefruit juice, but you wouldn't know it's there. Instead of providing a citrusy wallop, the flavors are overtly floral and botanical, with a hint of anise. It's so gorgeously intriguing it makes buying the bottle of Chartreuse entirely worth it. For a boozier cocktail, add ½ ounce (15 ml) gin, preferably New Western style, such as Thinking Tree (see Resources, page 172).

MAKES 1

1½ ounces (45 ml) Yellow Chartreuse (see Resources, page 171)

1½ ounces (45 ml) fresh grapefruit juice

3 ounces (90 ml) elderflower tonic water (preferably Q Mixers; see Resources, page 170) or half tonic, half prosecco, chilled

Grapefruit half-wheel, for garnish (see page 37)

Blossoming herb sprig such as thyme, or edible blossom such as borage, for garnish (see page 36)

Fill a wineglass three-quarters full with ice. Pour the Chartreuse and grapefruit juice over the ice. Add the tonic water and gently stir to combine. Tuck the grapefruit half-wheel between the ice and the glass and add the herb sprig or blossom.

ROSE OF PERSIA

Sweet, rich pomegranate with a floral touch

Rose flavors are often associated with Middle Eastern cuisine since rose syrup is a common addition to the desserts of the region. This juicy, fragrant pomegranate spritz takes its inspiration from that rich culinary tradition and gives you another way to use the rose syrup and rose water you can find at a Middle Eastern market.

MAKES 1

2 ounces (60 ml) unsweetened pomegranate juice

1 ounce (30 ml) Lillet Blanc aperitif (see Resources, page 171)

¼ ounce (7 ml) rose syrup (see Resources, page 172)

3 ounces (90 ml) sparkling rosé, chilled

½ teaspoon rose water

Lime peel, for garnish (see page 35)

Dried or fresh organic rosebud, for garnish (optional; see page 172)

Fill a wineglass three-quarters full with ice. Pour the pomegranate juice, Lillet, and rose syrup over the ice. Add the sparkling rosé and gently stir to combine. Add the rose water. Twist the lime peel over the drink and drop it in. Garnish with the rosebud, if using.

VARIATION

For a zero-proof drink, fill a wineglass three-quarters full with ice. Pour the pomegranate juice, rose syrup, and rose water over the ice. Add a squeeze of lime. Top with 4 ounces (120 ml) soda water or vanilla Dry Botanical Bubbly (see Resources, page 169). Gently stir to combine and garnish as directed.

THE BEAUREGARDE

For serious flower enthusiasts

This deeply lavender-hued and intensely floral spritz gets its over-the-top color and flavor thanks to crème de violette, a liqueur similar in flavor to French violet pastilles. A handful of fresh blueberries rounds out its strident floral notes beautifully.

MAKES 1

¼ cup (about 1¼ ounces/35 g) fresh blueberries

1¼ ounces (35 ml) crème de violette (see Resources, page 171)

2 ounces (60 ml) prosecco, chilled

1 to 2 ounces (30 to 60 ml) elderflower tonic water (preferably Q Mixers; see Resources, page 170), plain tonic water, or soda water, chilled

2 lemon wedges, 1 for garnish (see page 37)

Skewer of fresh blueberries, for garnish (see page 37)

Edible flower, such as a small chrysanthemum or sprig of fresh chamomile, for garnish (see page 37)

In a sturdy wineglass, muddle the blueberries with the crème de violette. Fill the glass three-quarters full with ice and stir. Add the prosecco and top with the elderflower tonic. Squeeze 1 lemon wedge into the drink and discard. Gently stir to combine. Cut a slit in the remaining lemon wedge and set on the rim of the glass. Garnish with the skewer of fresh blueberries and the edible flower.

Fizzy Water Field Guide

Sparkling water is the original "spritz" of a spritz. Diluting a drink—whether it's wine, spirits, or a mix—with a little bubbly water gives the drink a fizzy freshness without adding more alcohol and sugar. All unflavored sparkling waters can work interchangeably in a spritz, but they aren't all the same. Here's how to tell them apart.

Club soda: This force-carbonated beverage has a slightly salty flavor thanks to the addition of mineral salts like sodium or potassium bicarbonate meant to mimic the flavor of natural mineral water.

Seltzer, sparkling water, carbonated water, and soda water: These are different terms for the same thing—plain filtered water that's been carbonated, or made bubbly, by adding carbon dioxide under pressure. SodaStreams and soda siphons are tools for DIY carbonation. LaCroix and its ilk are the store-bought versions, and their assorted flavors can be fun to play with in a spritz.

Sparkling mineral water: Since this water comes from a natural spring or well, it has naturally occurring minerals that can impact the flavor. Some brands have naturally occurring bubbles, but most get their fizz from forced carbonation. Topo Chico, S.Pellegrino, and Perrier are a few familiar brands.

Tonic water: Unlike other bubbly waters, tonic water has added sugar, as well as a bittering agent like quinine. It's sometimes, but not always, interchangeable with sparkling water in a spritz. Just ask yourself if you want the added sweetness and tannic notes. Light tonic water is less sweet.

JAMAICAN ROSE

Petals upon petals

Dried hibiscus blossoms, called flor de Jamaica in Latin markets, brew up into a gorgeously ruby-red tea that's brisk, refreshing, and tart, like cranberry juice but not nearly as heavy. It goes exceptionally well with rose water, which lends an aromatic, floral complexity.

MAKES 1

3 ounces (90 ml) brewed and cooled hibiscus tea (see Note)

¾ ounce (20 ml) fresh lime juice

¾ ounce (20 ml) Simple Syrup (page 28)

3 ounces (90 ml) tonic water or vanilla Dry Botanical Bubbly (see Resources, page 169), chilled

¼ teaspoon rose water

Lime wheel, for garnish (see page 37)

Fill a wineglass three-quarters full with ice. Pour the hibiscus tea, lime juice, simple syrup, and tonic water over the ice. Gently stir to combine. Add the rose water and gently stir once more. Tuck the lime wheel between the ice and the glass.

NOTE: *To make the hibiscus tea, bring 2 cups (480 ml) water to a simmer in a saucepan. Add ¼ cup (60 ml) hibiscus tea (see Resources, page 172) and remove from the heat. Allow to steep for 10 minutes. Strain and refrigerate the tea until cold before using.*

Berries, cherries, peaches, and melons—these spritzes take full advantage of all the things we love best about spring and summer.

PRETTY IN PINK

For the strawberry-rhubarb fans

Not only is this light pink drink adorably fetching, but it also tastes like strawberry-rhubarb shortcake. The vanilla-flavored Dry sparkling soda adds a subtle, creamy, cake-batter note without going overboard on sweetness like a traditional cream soda, which would be just too sugary when combined with the strawberry-rhubarb syrup. Delicate and fruity Lillet Blanc supplies acidity and structure, while the cucumber garnish adds color and a breezy freshness.

MAKES 1

1 ounce (30 ml) Lillet Blanc aperitif (see Resources, page 171)

1 ounce (30 ml) Strawberry-Rhubarb Syrup (page 31)

2 ounces (60 ml) sparkling rosé, chilled

2 ounces (60 ml) vanilla Dry Botanical Bubbly (see Resources, page 169), chilled

Cucumber ribbon, for garnish (see page 36)

Fill a wineglass three-quarters full with ice. Pour the Lillet, simple syrup, sparkling rosé, and vanilla soda over the ice. Gently stir to combine. Tuck the cucumber ribbon between the ice and the side of the glass.

VARIATION

For a zero-proof drink, fill a wineglass three-quarters full with ice. Pour 2 ounces (60 ml) strawberry-rhubarb syrup, 2 ounces (60 ml) tonic or soda water, and 3 to 4 ounces (90 to 120 ml) vanilla Dry Botanical Bubbly over the ice. Add a squeeze of lime and garnish as directed.

APERCOT

Delicately apricotty

Sweet and fruity apricot nectar gets a subtle bitter twist with the addition of Aperol, and the gorgeous apricot color is a spirit-lifter all on its own. If you want the spritz a little sweeter, add the larger amount of nectar.

MAKES 1

1½ ounces (45 ml) Aperol
(see Resources, page 170)

1½ to 2 ounces (45 to 60 ml)
apricot nectar (see Resources,
page 170), chilled

½ ounce (15 ml) fresh lemon juice

2 ounces (60 ml) prosecco, chilled

1 ounce (30 ml) soda water, chilled

Thyme sprig, for garnish
(see page 36)

Edible flowers (like chamomile
blossoms), for garnish (optional;
see page 36)

Fill a wineglass three-quarters full with ice. Pour the Aperol, apricot nectar, lemon juice, and prosecco over the ice. Top with the soda water. Gently stir to combine. Garnish with the thyme sprig and float a few flowers on top, if using.

VARIATION

For a zero-proof drink, fill a wineglass three-quarters full with ice. Pour 3 ounces (90 ml) apricot nectar, ½ ounce (15 ml) fresh lemon juice, 2 ounces (60 ml) Sanbittèr soda (see Resources, page 170), and 2 ounces (60 ml) soda water over the ice. Gently stir to combine. Garnish as directed.

RASPBERRY BERET

Rich raspberries and fresh thyme transform sparkling rosé.

Raspberries have a jammy richness that can be overwhelming in a drink. To keep this spritz on the light and refreshing side, the raspberries are combined with cider vinegar to create a tangy shrub that adds brightness, while a splash of cucumber soda and herbal thyme supply notes of garden-freshness.

MAKES 1

1 ounce (30 ml) Lillet Blanc aperitif (see Resources, page 171)

¾ ounce (20 ml) Raspberry-Thyme Shrub (page 34)

¼ ounce (7 ml) Thyme Simple Syrup (page 29)

2 ounces (60 ml) sparkling rosé, chilled

1 ounce (30 ml) cucumber Dry Botanical Bubbly (see Resources, page 169), chilled

2 thyme sprigs, for garnish (see page 36)

Fill a wineglass three-quarters full with ice. Pour the Lillet, shrub, simple syrup, and sparkling rosé over the ice. Top with the cucumber soda. Gently stir to combine and garnish with the thyme sprigs.

VARIATION

For a zero-proof drink, fill a wineglass three-quarters full with ice. Pour 1½ ounces (45 ml) raspberry-thyme shrub, ¼ ounce (7 ml) thyme simple syrup, 1 ounce (30 ml) cucumber Dry Botanical Bubbly, and 3 ounces (90 ml) soda water over the ice. Gently stir to combine. Garnish as directed.

WATERMELONE

Your favorite agua fresca in spritz form

Watermelon agua fresca is the ideal summer drink. The combination of sweet watermelon juice, fresh lime, and a pinch of sugar is far more refreshing than the usual citrus suspects. A splash of tequila and a few glugs of prosecco are all you need to turn it into a spritz.

MAKES 1

2 mint sprigs

3 ounces (90 ml) watermelon juice (see Note), chilled

½ ounce (15 ml) Mint Simple Syrup (page 29), plus more (optional) to taste

½ ounce (15 ml) fresh lime juice

½ ounce (15 ml) tequila

2 ounces (60 ml) prosecco or sparkling rosé, chilled

1 lime wheel, for garnish (see page 37)

In a wineglass, muddle the leaves of 1 of the mint sprigs. Fill the glass three-quarters full with ice. Pour the watermelon juice, simple syrup, lime juice, tequila, and prosecco over the ice. Gently stir to combine. Taste and add more mint simple syrup, if desired. Tuck the lime wheel between the ice and the side of the glass. Garnish with the remaining mint sprig.

VARIATION

For a zero-proof drink, omit the tequila. Increase the lime juice to 1 ounce (30 ml) and substitute lime or plain sparkling water for the prosecco.

NOTE: *To make watermelon juice, puree chunks of seedless watermelon in a blender or food processor, then strain through a fine-mesh sieve. Two heaping cups of fruit (about 1 pound/455 g) will yield about 1¼ cups or 10 ounces (300 ml) of strained juice.*

BLUEBERRY LEMONADE SPRITZ

Put your bumper crop of blueberries to good use.

If you can't resist the yin and yang of tart lemons and sweet blueberries, you'll love this adorably pinky purple spritz. The muddled thyme adds an herbal dimension that makes it feel a little more grown-up.

MAKES 1

¼ cup (about 1¼ ounces/35 g) fresh blueberries

2 thyme sprigs

1 ounce (30 ml) fresh lemon juice

1 ounce (30 ml) Simple Syrup (plain, page 28; thyme, page 29; or honey, page 30)

3 ounces (90 ml) prosecco, chilled

1 ounce (30 ml) elderflower tonic water (preferably Q Mixers; see Resources, page 170), plain tonic water, or soda water, chilled

Skewered blueberries, for garnish (optional; see page 37)

In a sturdy wineglass, muddle the blueberries and 1 of the thyme sprigs. Fill the glass three-quarters full with ice and stir. Pour the lemon juice, simple syrup, and prosecco over the ice and top with the elderflower tonic. Gently stir to combine and garnish with the remaining thyme sprig and the skewer of blueberries, if using.

VARIATION

For a zero-proof drink, replace the prosecco with additional elderflower tonic or with lemon sparkling water.

PEACHY KEEN

A touch of nutty amaretto
brings out the lush flavor of fresh peaches.

No store-bought juice can beat the flavor of fresh peach in this Lillet-based spritz. But it's not easy to sip around big chunks of fresh fruit. The trick is to muddle a generous amount of peeled peach until juicy, then strain out the fruit. A little herby basil enhances the summery flavor, while the tiniest hint of amaretto adds a lush nuttiness. Just be sure your peaches are dripping-ripe. Nectarines work perfectly too.

MAKES 1

½ large (about 4-ounce/115 g)
ripe peach, peeled

2 basil sprigs

1½ ounces (45 ml) Lillet Blanc
aperitif (see Resources, page 171)

½ ounce (15 ml) amaretto

4 ounces (120 ml) prosecco, chilled

Peach wedge, for garnish
(see page 37)

In a mixing glass or cocktail shaker, muddle the peach and the leaves from 1 of the basil sprigs. Add the Lillet, amaretto, and a handful of ice. Stir until cold, about 20 seconds. Fill a wineglass three-quarters full with ice. Strain the Lillet mixture over the ice, then add the prosecco. Gently stir to combine and garnish with the remaining basil sprig and the peach wedge.

SANGRIA SPRITZ

A party in a glass

Spanish sangria is like fruit punch for grown-ups—and just as irresistible on a hot summer day as that sounds. Here it's given the spritz treatment with sparkling Lambrusco as the base and Aperol adding fruity sweetness and a bitter bite in one fell swoop. With its easy-to-remember ratio, this spritz is as perfect for parties as it is for lazy afternoons. Mix it in a large glass so there's plenty of room for all those wine-soaked fruits.

MAKES 1

2 ounces (60 ml) Aperol
(see Resources, page 170)

3 ounces (90 ml) dry Lambrusco,
chilled

2 ounces (60 ml) soda water,
chilled

1 peach wedge, diced
(about 1 ounce/30 g)

1 apple wedge, diced
(about ½ ounce/15 g)

1 lime wedge

1 orange half-wheel, for garnish
(see page 37)

1 lemon and/or lime wheel,
for garnish (see page 37)

Fill a tumbler or goblet-sized wineglass half full with ice. Pour the Aperol and Lambrusco over the ice. Top with the soda water. Gently stir to combine. Add the diced peach and diced apple. Squeeze the lime wedge into the glass and drop it in. Gently stir again to distribute. Tuck the orange and lemon and/or lime wheel between the ice and the side of the glass.

DR CHERRY

Dr Pepper meets Cherry Coke.

Try this spritz and decide if it tastes more like cherry cola or Dr Pepper. Suffice it to say, if you like either one of those soft drinks, you'll love this spritz. The sparkling cherry juice really makes it, but if you can't find it, you can use ¾ ounce (20 ml) tart cherry juice and 2 ounces (60 ml) sparkling apple cider instead. For a boozier drink, add ½ ounce (15 ml) bourbon.

MAKES 1

1½ ounces (45 ml) Bonal Gentiane-Quina aperitif (see Resources, page 171) or Amaro Averna (see Resources, page 170)

2 ounces (60 ml) prosecco, chilled

2 ounces (60 ml) Knudsen sparkling cherry juice (see Resources, page 170), chilled

1 lemon wedge

1 ounce (30 ml) vanilla Dry Botanical Bubbly (see Resources, page 169) or plain soda water, chilled

Lemon wheel, for garnish (see page 37)

Fill a wineglass three-quarters full with ice. Pour the Bonal, prosecco, and sparkling cherry juice over the ice. Squeeze the lemon wedge into the drink and discard. Top with the soda water and gently stir to combine. Tuck the lemon wheel between the ice and the side of the glass.

VARIATION

For a zero-proof drink, fill a wineglass three-quarters full with ice. Pour 1½ ounces (45 ml) Sanbittèr soda (see Resources, page 170), 2 ounces (60 ml) sparkling apple cider, 1½ ounces (45 ml) tart cherry juice, and 1½ ounces (45 ml) vanilla Dry Botanical Bubbly over the ice. Gently stir to combine. Garnish as directed.

CANTALOUPE + FENNEL

HOLD THE BOOZE

A touch of anise adds intrigue to the mild-mannered melon.

Juicy, mildly sweet cantaloupe and aromatic fennel come together beautifully in this breezy-fresh zero-proof spritz. You can use fresh fennel (¼ cup/30 g thinly sliced) for a very subtle hint of anise flavor, but the seeds are easier to muddle and the flavor a touch stronger. Don't worry; it's still just a subtle hint of licorice, and the tonic water adds welcome bitter notes. Even if you're not a fan of anise flavors, you'll love this drink.

MAKES 1

1 teaspoon fennel seeds

1 cup (about 4 ounces/115 g) cubed ripe cantaloupe

½ ounce (15 ml) fresh lime juice

½ ounce (15 ml) Simple Syrup (page 28)

2 to 3 ounces (60 to 90 ml) tonic water, chilled

1 to 3 cantaloupe balls, for garnish

Fennel frond, for garnish (see page 36)

In a mixing glass or cocktail shaker, muddle the fennel seeds to bruise them. Add the cantaloupe and muddle until the fruit is fully mashed. Fill a wineglass three-quarters full with ice. Strain the cantaloupe mixture over the ice, pressing on the solids to extract the liquid. Add the lime juice and simple syrup and top with the tonic water (use the lesser amount for a fruitier flavor, the larger amount for more bitter notes). Gently stir to combine. Float the cantaloupe balls on top. Garnish with the fennel frond.

Bright, citrusy sippers and lush sparklers with tropical vibes—when you have one of these in hand, there's no such thing as a gloomy day.

ANNETTE LIMONCELLO

Cheerful and bubbly

One cannot live by orange spritzes alone. When you crave a different sort of citrus, reach for limoncello. Here it's transformed from a bittersweet aperitif into a light, lemony, and bubbly refresher with just a hint of mint.

MAKES 1

1 ounce (30 ml) limoncello (see Note)

½ ounce (15 ml) Mint Simple Syrup (page 29)

3 ounces (90 ml) prosecco, chilled

2 ounces (60 ml) soda water, chilled

1 lemon wedge

Lemon wheel, for garnish (see page 37)

Mint sprig, for garnish (see page 36)

Fill a wineglass three-quarters full with ice. Pour the limoncello, simple syrup, and prosecco over the ice. Top with the soda water. Squeeze the lemon wedge into the drink and discard. Gently stir to combine. Tuck the lemon wheel between the ice and the side of the glass and garnish with the mint sprig.

NOTE: *To make limoncello yourself, combine the peels of 10 lemons (just the yellow part, no white pith) with one 750 ml bottle of vodka in a large jar with a lid and allow it to infuse in a cool, dark place for 1 month. Strain and add 1 to 2 cups (240 to 480 ml) of Simple Syrup (page 28), or more to taste. More simple syrup will dilute the alcohol, however, so if you want to avoid that but still make it sweeter, prepare a richer simple syrup with a higher ratio of sugar to water.*

CANARY BIRD

A tonic for the mind and the senses

This passion-fruity spritz is named for its bright color, but it also includes three important letters: CBD. (Plus, if you find yourself needing more than one of these a night, that's your canary-in-a-coal-mine sign that you might be overstressed.) Although not yet legal in every state, CBD oil (the kind without the psychotropic compound THC) won't get you high, but its calming and anti-inflammatory properties can do wonders to relieve muscle pain, headaches, and the tension of a busy day. Here CBD oil and turmeric work together to reduce inflammation and relieve stress, while orange, lime, and passion fruit mingle into a bright and uplifting drink. Flavor-wise, the oil doesn't make or break the drink, so leave it out if you like.

MAKES 1

1½ ounces (45 ml) Cappelletti Aperitivo Americano or Aperol (see Resources, page 170), or ½ ounce (15 ml) of each

1 ounce (30 ml) passion fruit puree

½ ounce (15 ml) fresh lime juice

1 dropper of unflavored or citrus-flavored CBD oil (35 mg per serving)

¼ teaspoon turmeric

3 to 4 ounces (90 to 120 ml) Sanpellegrino Aranciata or Aranciata Rossa orange soda (see Resources, page 170), chilled

Orange wheel, for garnish (see page 37)

Fill a wineglass three-quarters full with ice. Pour the Cappelletti, passion fruit puree, and lime juice over the ice. Add the CBD oil and turmeric. Gently stir to combine. Top with the orange soda. Gently stir once more. Tuck the orange wheel between the ice and the side of the glass.

VARIATION

For a zero-proof drink, omit the Cappelletti.

JUST A SPRITZ
94

CAPPELLETTI SHANDY

Hoppy beer and grapefruit are made for each other.

Nothing quenches thirst on a hot day like a super-citrusy juicy IPA—except one that's mixed with a big splash of grapefruit juice. This spritzified version of a shandy (beer mixed with a nonalcoholic drink, like lemonade or juice) gets its lighter and fizzier feel thanks to grapefruit-infused sparkling water, then incorporates Cappelletti for a bit more structure without adding significant bitterness to compete with the hops in the beer. A dash of orange or grapefruit bitters enhances all that citrus.

MAKES 1

1½ ounces (45 ml) Cappelletti Aperitivo Americano (see Resources, page 170)

3½ ounces (105 ml) juicy IPA beer, such as Ninkasi Prismatic (see Resources, page 171), chilled

2 ounces (60 ml) grapefruit sparkling water, preferably Spindrift (see Resources, page 170), chilled

Dash of grapefruit or orange bitters (see Resources, page 169)

Grapefruit half-wheel or orange wheel, for garnish (see page 37)

Fill a wineglass three-quarters full with ice. Pour the Cappelletti, beer, and grapefruit sparkling water over the ice. Gently stir to combine. Top with the bitters and tuck the citrus wheel between the ice and the side of the glass.

MARGARITA SPRITZ

Just add chips and guac.

Chile-spiced or strawberry sweet, smoky or stinging with habanero heat, there isn't a style of margarita that can't be re-created in spritz form. This classic margarita spritz is fizzy and low alcohol, and it will soon be your favorite type of marg. The recipe uses tonic water instead of prosecco or soda water, which adds the requisite bubbles without making the drink taste winey or watered down.

MAKES 1

1 ounce (30 ml) tequila or mezcal (or ½ ounce/15 ml of each)

1 ounce (30 ml) fresh lime juice

½ ounce (15 ml) fresh orange juice

½ ounce (15 ml) Simple Syrup (page 28)

3 ounces (90 ml) tonic water, chilled

Pinch of kosher salt

2 to 3 dashes of orange bitters (see Resources, page 169)

Lime wheel, for garnish (see page 37)

Orange wheel, for garnish (see page 37)

Fill a wineglass three-quarters full with ice. Pour the tequila, lime juice, orange juice, simple syrup, and tonic water over the ice. Add the salt and gently stir to combine. Add the bitters and tuck the lime and orange wheels between the ice and the side of the glass.

VARIATION
For an almost zero-proof drink, omit the tequila.

SUNRISE BAY

Love this journey for you

Named in honor of a certain fictional soap opera, this spritz tastes like a passion fruit Creamsicle but looks like a tequila sunrise—two wonderfully kitschy delights in one.

MAKES 1

1½ ounces (45 ml) passion fruit puree

1 ounce (30 ml) Vanilla Simple Syrup (page 29), plus more (optional) to taste

1 lime wedge

2 ounces (60 ml) prosecco, chilled

2 ounces (60 ml) coconut-flavored sparkling water, chilled

¼ ounce (7 ml) grenadine

Orange wheel, for garnish (see page 37)

Maraschino cherry, for garnish

Fill a wineglass three-quarters full with ice. Pour the passion fruit puree and simple syrup over the ice. Squeeze the lime wedge into the drink and discard. Top with the prosecco and sparkling water. Gently stir to combine. Add the grenadine, which will sink to the bottom. Taste and add more simple syrup, if desired. Skewer the orange wheel and cherry together and set on top to garnish.

VARIATION

For a zero-proof drink, fill a wineglass three-quarters full with ice. Pour 3 to 4 ounces (90 to 120 ml) coconut sparkling water, the juice from 1 lime wedge, 1½ ounces (45 ml) passion fruit puree, and ½ ounce (15 ml) vanilla simple syrup over the ice. Gently stir to combine. Add ¼ ounce (7 ml) grenadine and garnish as directed.

LILLET AND LEMON

A lemon lift for a lightly sweet aperitif

More herbal and lighter than the Annette Limoncello (page 93), this pleasantly bitter and lemony spritz refreshes like no other. I love the juicy flavor of Spindrift lemon sparkling water, but any similarly flavored brand will do. If you want the drink a little sweeter, add more simple syrup to taste.

MAKES 1

2 ounces (60 ml) Lillet Blanc aperitif (see Resources, page 171)

1/2 ounce (15 ml) gin, preferably New Western style, such as Thinking Tree (see Resources, page 172)

1/2 ounce (15 ml) fresh lemon juice

1/2 ounce (15 ml) Basil Simple Syrup (page 29)

2 ounces (60 ml) prosecco, chilled

1 to 2 ounces (30 to 60 ml) lemon sparkling water, preferably Spindrift (see Resources, page 170), chilled

Lemon wheel, for garnish (see page 37)

Basil sprig, for garnish (see page 36)

Fill a wineglass three-quarters full with ice. Pour the Lillet, gin, lemon juice, simple syrup, and prosecco over the ice. Top with the sparkling water. Gently stir to combine. Tuck the lemon wheel between the ice and the side of the glass and garnish with the basil sprig.

GRAPEFRUIT SPRITZ

A juiced-up riff on the Venetian classic

Grapefruits are such a wonder. Their natural bitterness seems perfectly calibrated to balance their tart piquancy and almost floral sweetness, making them perhaps the most refreshing citrus on the planet. They're a natural addition to a spritz, especially the Ruby Red varieties.

MAKES 1

1½ ounces (45 ml) Aperol or Campari (see Resources, page 170), or ¾ ounce (20 ml) of each

3 ounces (90 ml) fresh pink grapefruit juice, chilled

2 ounces (60 ml) prosecco, chilled

1 ounce (30 ml) grapefruit flavor or plain soda water, chilled

Dash of grapefruit or orange bitters (see Resources, page 169)

Grapefruit half-wheel, for garnish (see page 37)

Fill a wineglass three-quarters full with ice. Pour the Aperol, grapefruit juice, and prosecco over the ice. Top with the soda water. Gently stir to combine. Add the bitters and tuck the grapefruit half-wheel between the ice and the side of the glass.

VARIATION

For a zero-proof drink, fill a wineglass three-quarters full with ice. Pour 2 ounces (60 ml) Sanbittèr soda (see Resources, page 170), 3 ounces (90 ml) grapefruit juice, and 3 ounces (90 ml) tonic water over the ice. Gently stir to combine and garnish as directed.

THE STARBURST

A juicy orange spritz

We all know that the best Starburst candy is the orange one, right? Right? Well, even if you don't agree, as long as you like orange flavors, you'll love this spritz. This is the drink to serve to friends who aren't up for anything too tannic, and the proportions are very easy to remember. The blood orange soda makes it super juicy and downplays the bitterness of the Aperol. If you can handle a bit more bite, use Campari instead of Aperol.

MAKES 1

2 ounces (60 ml) Aperol or Campari (see Resources, page 170)

2 ounces (60 ml) Sanpellegrino Aranciata or Aranciata Rossa orange soda (see Resources, page 170), chilled

2 ounces (60 ml) prosecco, chilled

Blood orange wheel, for garnish (see page 37)

Fill a wineglass three-quarters full with ice. Pour the Aperol, orange soda, and prosecco over the ice. Gently stir to combine. Tuck the orange wheel between the ice and the side of the glass.

GINGER'S ISLAND

A spicy twist on a rum, pineapple, and orange classic

Think of this as a light and fizzy planter's punch with a spicy ginger bite. It's sweet and tropical in a come-hither red. No doubt, Gilligan and the rest of the castaways would approve.

MAKES 1

2 ounces (60 ml) pineapple juice, chilled

1 ounce (30 ml) amber rum, preferably Appleton Estate Reserve (see Resources, page 170)

½ ounce (15 ml) fresh lime juice

½ ounce (15 ml) fresh orange juice

¼ teaspoon grated fresh ginger

2 ounces (60 ml) sparkling rosé or prosecco, chilled

2 ounces (60 ml) ginger beer, preferably Q Mixers (see Resources, page 170)

½ ounce (15 ml) grenadine

Dash of Angostura bitters (see Resources, page 169)

Skewer of pineapple chunks and maraschino cherries, for garnish (see page 37)

Mint sprig, for garnish (optional; see page 36)

Fill a large wineglass three-quarters full with ice. Pour the pineapple juice, rum, lime juice, and orange juice over the ice. Add the ginger and stir. Add the sparkling rosé and top with the ginger beer. Add the grenadine and let it sink to the bottom. Add the bitters and garnish with the skewer of pineapples and cherries, and the mint sprig, if using.

VARIATION

For an almost zero-proof drink, omit the rum and sparkling wine and double the ginger beer.

YACHT ROCK

Send your troubles sailing away on a fizzy pineapple-coconut sea.

If you like piña coladas . . . then put this spritz on your must-make list. It's brighter and lighter than the classic creamy tiki drink but with all the lush coconut flavors you crave. Coconut-flavored sparkling water and a bit of vanilla simple syrup provide the perfect stand-ins for thick coconut cream.

MAKES 1

3 ounces (90 ml) pineapple juice, chilled

½ ounce (15 ml) Aperol (see Resources, page 170)

½ ounce (15 ml) fresh lime juice

¼ ounce (7 ml) Vanilla Simple Syrup (page 29)

2 ounces (60 ml) sparkling rosé or prosecco, chilled

2 ounces (60 ml) coconut-flavored sparkling water, chilled

Pineapple triangle, for garnish (see page 36)

2 or 3 pineapple leaves, for garnish (see page 36)

Fill a wineglass three-quarters full with ice. Pour the pineapple juice, Aperol, lime juice, and simple syrup over the ice. Add the sparkling rosé and top with the sparkling water. Gently stir to combine. Cut a slit in the point of the pineapple triangle and set it on the rim of the glass. Garnish with the pineapple leaves.

VARIATION

For a zero-proof drink, fill a wineglass three-quarters full with ice. Pour 2 ounces (60 ml) coconut sparkling water, 3 ounces (90 ml) pineapple juice, ½ ounce (15 ml) fresh lime juice, and 1 ounce (30 ml) Sanbittèr soda (see Resources, page 170) or Lurisia chinotto (see Resources, page 169) over the ice. Gently stir to combine and garnish as directed.

VAGUELY TIKI

Tropical and complex but without all the fuss

Tiki drinks are not easily made at home—at least not without a large arsenal of spirits and syrups. And yet when you're craving something tropical and spiced and easy to mix up, this spritz should do the trick. Instead of getting its layer of rich nuttiness from orgeat syrup (a mixture of almonds, sugar, and orange blossom water common in tiki drinks), it uses amaretto liqueur, which is easier to find, lasts indefinitely, and is a versatile addition to any home bar. Use the greater amount if you want the drink more lush and nutty.

MAKES 1

1 ounce (30 ml) mango juice, chilled

¾ ounce (20 ml) amber rum, preferably Appleton Estate Reserve (see Resources, page 170)

½ to ¾ ounce (15 to 20 ml) amaretto

½ ounce (15 ml) curaçao or triple sec, such as Cointreau

½ ounce (15 ml) fresh lime juice

4 ounces (120 ml) prosecco or sparkling rosé, chilled

3 dashes Angostura bitters (see Resources, page 169)

Umbrella-skewered maraschino cherries or swizzle stick with lime peel sails, for garnish (see page 35)

Fill a wineglass three-quarters full with ice. Pour the mango juice, rum, amaretto, curaçao, lime juice, and prosecco over the ice. Gently stir to combine and add the bitters and garnish.

CURRY FAVOR

HOLD THE BOOZE

Lush, coconutty, and fragrant

Many of the same fresh herbs used in Thai curries make for a fabulously refreshing and aromatic tropical spritz. Redolent makrut lime leaves and lemongrass lend a vibrant citrus aroma, with ginger and Thai chile adding a warm glow of heat. A little coconut cream skimmed off the top of a can of coconut milk enriches the drink without weighing it down, and it gets a flavor assist from coconut sparkling water. You can get the herbs and chile at well-stocked groceries or Asian markets.

MAKES 1

2 small makrut lime leaves, one minced and one reserved for garnish

½-inch (1 cm) piece of fresh ginger, peeled and minced

½-inch (1 cm) piece of lemongrass, cut from the root end, minced

½ Thai chile (seeds removed for less heat)

2 teaspoons (10 ml) unsweetened coconut cream

1 ounce (30 ml) fresh lime juice

1 ounce (30 ml) Simple Syrup (page 28)

4 to 6 ounces (120 to 175 ml) coconut-flavored sparkling water, chilled

Dash of Peychaud's bitters (optional; see Resources, page 169)

Stalk of lemongrass, for garnish (see page 36)

Lime wheel, for garnish (see page 37)

In a mixing glass or cocktail shaker, muddle the minced lime leaf, ginger, minced lemongrass, chile, coconut cream, lime juice, and simple syrup until the solids are fully mashed. Fill a wineglass three-quarters full with ice. Strain the mixture over the ice, pressing on the solids to extract the liquid. Top with the coconut sparkling water (use the lesser amount for a richer drink). Gently stir to combine. Add the bitters, if using. Cut the lemongrass so that it's about an inch (3 cm) taller than the glass. Cut a slit in the top of the stalk and insert the remaining lime leaf. Add to the glass along with the lime wheel for garnish.

BITTER IS BEAUTIFUL

Bitter gets a bad rap. Without it, there is no sweet, and there's no substitute for the way it slaps your palate awake. This chapter takes off the kid gloves. If you're uninitiated in the power of assertive flavors, just take it slow and be open to the possibilities.

THE CUCUMBERBATCH

Flinty yet approachable

Cool and breezy cucumber combines with a touch of gin and the minerally, almost saline flavor of Mattei Cap Corse Blanc to create a super-light and refreshing spritz reminiscent of a gin and tonic.

MAKES 1

1/3 cup (about 2 ounces/55 g) peeled, sliced, seeded cucumber

1 1/2 to 2 ounces (45 to 60 ml) Mattei Cap Corse Blanc (see Resources, page 171)

1/4 ounce (7 ml) gin, preferably New Western style, such as Thinking Tree (see Resources, page 172)

2 to 3 ounces (60 to 90 ml) cucumber Dry Botanical Bubbly (see Resources, page 169), chilled

2 lime wedges, 1 for garnish (see page 37)

Skewered cucumber ribbon, for garnish (see page 36)

In a mixing glass or cocktail shaker, muddle the sliced cucumber with the Cap Corse Blanc. Fill a wineglass three-quarters full with ice. Strain the cucumber mixture over the ice, pressing on the solids to extract the liquid. Add the gin and sparkling soda. Squeeze 1 lime wedge into the drink and discard. Gently stir to combine. Cut a slit in the remaining lime wedge and set on the rim of the glass. Garnish with the cucumber ribbon.

VARIATION

For a zero-proof drink, fill a wineglass three-quarters full with ice. In a mixing glass or cocktail shaker, muddle the cucumber with 1/4 ounce (7 ml) lime juice, 1 ounce (30 ml) Seedlip Garden 108 (see Resources, page 171), and 1/4 ounce (7 ml) Thyme Simple Syrup (page 29). Pour the mixture over the ice and top with 2 ounces (60 ml) cucumber Dry Botanical Bubbly or tonic water. Gently stir to combine and garnish as directed.

CYNAR-BERRY

Bold cranberry mingles with bittersweet Cynar.

Skip the cranberry cocktail juice and go for the full-strength option for this one. Cynar's herbal, honey-like sweetness is all you need to offset cranberry's natural tannic tartness. If you need to sweeten it up, add a little simple syrup to taste or use cranberry juice cocktail and only 2 ounces (60 ml) of prosecco.

MAKES 1

3 ounces (90 ml) unsweetened 100 percent cranberry juice, chilled

1 ounce (30 ml) Cynar (see Resources, page 170)

4 ounces (120 ml) prosecco, chilled

Lemon peel, for garnish (see page 35)

Fill a wineglass three-quarters full with ice. Pour the cranberry juice, Cynar, and prosecco over the ice. Gently stir to combine. Twist the lemon peel over the drink and drop it in.

VARIATION

For a zero-proof drink, fill a wineglass three-quarters full with ice. Pour 3 ounces (90 ml) Lurisia chinotto (see Resources, page 169), 1½ ounces (45 ml) unsweetened cranberry juice, a squeeze of lime, and 1 to 2 ounces (30 to 60 ml) tonic water over the ice. Gently stir to combine. Taste and add a splash of simple syrup, if desired, and garnish as directed.

VA-VA-VERMOUTH

Sweet vermouth takes center stage.

This spritz highlights the burnt-sugar, dark-caramel flavors of sweet vermouth. A squeeze of fresh grapefruit juice aligns with the vermouth's bittersweetness and gives it just enough juicy brightness to balance those rich flavors.

MAKES 1

2 ounces (60 ml) sweet vermouth, such as Carpano Antica Formula or Punt e Mes (see Resources, page 171)

½ ounce (15 ml) fresh pink grapefruit juice

2 ounces (60 ml) prosecco, chilled

1 ounce (30 ml) soda water, chilled

Grapefruit half-wheel, for garnish (see page 37)

Fill a wineglass three-quarters full with ice. Pour the vermouth, grapefruit juice, and prosecco over the ice. Top with the soda water and gently stir to combine. Tuck the grapefruit half-wheel between the ice and the side of the glass.

VARIATION

For a zero-proof drink, fill a wineglass three-quarters full with ice. Combine 3 ounces (90 ml) Lurisia chinotto (see Resources, page 169) and 3 ounces (90 ml) grapefruit juice over the ice. Gently stir to combine and garnish as directed.

Bitter Before Dinner?

According to generations of Europeans, the tradition of sipping an aperitif of amaro and soda before dinner will stimulate the appetite—and a couple hundred years of the practice is confirmation enough for some. But things are a bit more complex than that.

Bitter tastes do indeed trigger bitter receptors in the mouth to produce saliva, and when your juices are flowing, you'll feel more geared up to eat. Bitter tastes are also a digestive stimulant, activating bitter receptors in the gastrointestinal tract, which trigger digestive hormones and secretions like bile to help break down nutrients. Finally, scientific proof of the efficacy of digestivos!

Since bitter things are often toxic, these secretions are the body's way of helping you flush things out in case you ingested something you shouldn't have. And that's why these helpful receptors also trigger the secretion of a satiety hormone that tells your brain to stop eating.

But wait . . . isn't that pretty much the opposite of an appetite stimulant? Does that mean we should skip a fizzed-up amaro before dinner after all? Absolutely not. In fact, it's probably wise to sip before a big feast. The bitter flavors get your palate revved up, but they'll then interact with your gut and tell your brain to go easy, so there's less chance you'll overeat. Win-win.

SWEET THISTLE

A blood orange beauty

Here the lovely bitter-honey flavor of Cynar gets the spotlight, fizzed up with splashes of prosecco and soda water.

MAKES 1

1½ ounces (45 ml) Cynar (see Resources, page 170)

¾ ounce (20 ml) fresh blood orange or regular orange juice

3 ounces (90 ml) prosecco, chilled

1½ ounces (45 ml) soda water, chilled

Blood orange wheel, for garnish (see page 37)

Rosemary sprig, for garnish (see page 36)

Fill a wineglass three-quarters full with ice. Pour the Cynar, blood orange juice, and prosecco over the ice. Top with the soda water and gently stir to combine. Tuck the orange wheel between the ice and the side of the glass. Garnish with the rosemary sprig.

VARIATION

For a zero-proof drink, fill a wineglass three-quarters full with ice. Pour 2 ounces (60 ml) fresh blood orange juice or fresh orange juice, 2 ounces (60 ml) Lurisia chinotto or Sanbittèr soda (see Resources, page 170), ½ ounce (15 ml) fresh lemon juice, and 1 ounce (30 ml) tonic water over the ice. Gently stir to combine. Garnish as directed.

TEA GARDEN

Herbaceous and fresh

Iced green tea and basil syrup echo the cavalcade of bracing herbs in the Yellow Chartreuse, making every sip of this taste like walking through an herb garden on a cool spring day. It's refreshing and light yet pleasantly bitter, with just enough caffeine from the tea to keep you on your feet. I like using key limes for this because they're just a bit more aromatic, but regular limes will certainly work.

MAKES 1

3 ounces (90 ml) unsweetened green tea, chilled

1 ounce (30 ml) Yellow Chartreuse (see Resources, page 171)

½ ounce (15 ml) Basil Simple Syrup (page 29)

¼ ounce (7 ml) fresh lime juice

2 ounces (60 ml) prosecco, chilled

2 ounces (60 ml) soda water, chilled

Lime wedge, for garnish (see page 37)

Basil sprig, for garnish (see page 36)

Fill a wineglass three-quarters full with ice. Pour the green tea, Yellow Chartreuse, simple syrup, lime juice, and prosecco over the ice. Top with the soda water and gently stir to combine. Garnish with the lime wedge and basil sprig.

VARIATION

For a zero-proof drink, omit the Chartreuse and prosecco. Add ½ ounce (15 ml) Seedlip Garden 108 (see Resources, page 171). You can also substitute tonic water for the soda water.

COLD BREW FRIZZANTE

The ultimate pick-me-up

In Sicily, little cups of sweet, icy coffee granita topped with a dollop of whipped cream are a popular way to both cool off and get an afternoon pick-me-up. This spritzy take plays in the same sandbox and provides a great backdrop for Sicilian Amaro Averna. I like to make cold brew for this, with a chocolatey bean like Sumatra and a bit of fennel seed added to the coffee grounds to echo the flavors of Averna. The result is gorgeously aromatic, rich yet fresh and sweet, and ideal for brunch.

MAKES 1

2 ounces (60 ml) cold brew coffee (see Note) or cooled espresso

1 ounce (30 ml) Amaro Averna (see Resources, page 170) or Bonal Gentiane-Quina aperitif (see Resources, page 171)

½ ounce (15 ml) Vanilla Simple Syrup (page 29)

2 ounces (60 ml) soda water, chilled

Orange half-wheel, for garnish (see page 37)

Softly whipped cream, for garnish

Fill a wineglass three-quarters full with ice. Pour the coffee, Averna, simple syrup, and soda water over the ice. Gently stir to combine. Tuck the orange half-wheel between the ice and the side of the glass. Garnish with a dollop of softly whipped cream.

VARIATION

For a zero-proof drink, replace the Averna with Lurisia chinotto (see Resources, page 169) and the soda water with tonic water.

NOTE: *To make cold brew, combine ½ cup (50 g) coarse-ground coffee and 1½ teaspoons fennel seeds with 4 cups (960 ml) cold filtered water. Allow to steep for 12 hours. Strain and refrigerate.*

WHITE NEGRONI
SBAGLIATO

A change of pace for Negroni lovers

Swapping out the Campari for Suze and the red (sweet) vermouth for white (dry) vermouth results in what's called a White Negroni (though it's really quite yellow). It's a delicious change of pace from the original bitter orange flavor profile—more herbal and grapefruity but just as bracing. For this spritzified version, skip the gin and use a sweeter aromatized wine instead of the dry vermouth. I prefer the sweeter profile of Cocchi Americano for this, but if you want an even more bitter and herbal option, try Mattei Cap Corse Blanc (see Resources, page 171) and add a splash of soda water. Suze is powerfully flavored stuff, so start with the lesser amount listed, taste, and add more if you like.

MAKES 1

1 ounce (30 ml) Cocchi Americano Bianco aperitif (see Resources, page 171)

¾ to 1 ounce (20 to 30 ml) Suze aperitif (see Resources, page 170)

3 ounces (90 ml) prosecco, chilled

A few dashes of grapefruit bitters (see Resources, page 169)

Grapefruit half-wheel, for garnish (see page 37)

Fill a wineglass three-quarters full with ice. Pour the Cocchi Americano, Suze, and prosecco over the ice. Gently stir to combine. Add the bitters and tuck the grapefruit half-wheel between the ice and the side of the glass.

SO PITHY

Lemonade with an herbal punch

You can characterize this mouthwatering spritz as sparkling lemonade that's been given a big slap of savory, herbal bitterness. It's just the ticket with a bowl of salty Marcona almonds.

MAKES 1

1½ ounces (45 ml) Mattei Cap Corse Blanc (see Resources, page 171)

¾ ounce (20 ml) fresh lemon juice

¾ ounce (20 ml) Thyme Simple Syrup (page 29)

½ ounce (15 ml) gin, preferably New Western style, such as Thinking Tree (see Resources, page 172)

2 ounces (60 ml) prosecco, chilled

Lemon wheel, for garnish (see page 37)

Thyme sprig, for garnish (see page 36)

Fill a wineglass three-quarters full with ice. Pour the Cap Corse Blanc, lemon juice, simple syrup, gin, and prosecco over the ice. Gently stir to combine. Tuck the lemon wheel between the ice and the side of the glass. Garnish with the thyme sprig.

CELERY-MINT SPRITZ

Salty and savory, yet cool and breezy

Fresh celery juice is fantastic in a spritz, with lemon juice for brightness and tonic for that kick of quinine bitterness. The muddled mint makes the whole drink that much fresher and breezier, but you can skip it for a more pronounced celery flavor.

MAKES 1

3 large (about 8 ounces/225 g) celery stalks, ends trimmed

1 ounce (30 ml) lemon juice

1 ounce (30 ml) Simple Syrup (page 28), plus more (optional) to taste

2 mint sprigs

2 ounces (60 ml) tonic water, chilled

1 lemon wedge, for garnish (see page 37)

Juice the celery in a vegetable juicer or roughly chop and use a food processor or an immersion blender to puree it with the lemon juice and simple syrup (there's not enough liquid for a regular blender to work well). Strain through a fine-mesh sieve, pressing to extract the juice. You will need 3 ounces (90 ml) of liquid (save any extra juice for another serving, or drink it straight).

In a sturdy wineglass, muddle the leaves of 1 mint sprig. Fill the glass three-quarters full with ice. Pour the celery juice, lemon juice and simple syrup (if not already added), and tonic water over the ice. Gently stir to combine. Squeeze the lemon wedge into the glass and drop it in. Taste and add more simple syrup, if desired. Garnish with the remaining mint sprig.

You don't have to stop spritzing when summer's over. Wintry fruits and warm baking spices take well to bubbly wines and set the stage for all the parties and feasts of the season. You can even batch up the spirits and juices and keep them cold until guests arrive. Then pop the cork and let the drinks flow.

THE BIG BIRD

A cran-orange sipper ideal for fall and winter feasts

This easy-drinking, easy-to-make spritz is reminiscent of the cranberry sauce served at Thanksgiving, in the best possible way. For less bitterness, use cranberry juice cocktail instead of unsweetened. The rosemary sprig garnish is nonnegotiable; it adds an aromatic hit of herbal freshness.

MAKES 1

2 ounces (60 ml) Aperol
(see Resources, page 170)

2 ounces (60 ml) unsweetened
100 percent cranberry juice,
chilled

4 ounces (120 ml) prosecco,
chilled

Rosemary sprig, for garnish
(see page 36)

Whole cranberries, for garnish

Fill a wineglass three-quarters full with ice. Pour the Aperol, cranberry juice, and prosecco over the ice. Gently stir to combine. Garnish with the rosemary sprig and float a few cranberries on top.

VARIATION

For a zero-proof drink, fill a wineglass three-quarters full with ice. Combine 1½ ounces (45 ml) cranberry juice, 2 ounces (60 ml) Crodino (see Resources, page 169), ¼ ounce (7 ml) Thyme or Rosemary Simple Syrup (page 29), and 4 ounces (120 ml) soda water over the ice. Gently stir to combine and garnish as directed.

THE NUTCRACKER

Well-aged sherry adds nutty richness to bright cranberry.

Bitter, tart cranberry juice works together with the aged sherry to create a lush spritz that tastes a lot more complicated than it is. If unsweetened cranberry juice is just too tannic for you, feel free to use cranberry juice cocktail. The drink will taste more juicy and less nutty, so increase the sherry to 2 ounces (60 ml). You may need more or less simple syrup, depending on how sweet the juice is. Just start with the lesser amount and add more until the drink is to your liking.

MAKES 1

1½ ounces (45 ml) amontillado or oloroso sherry

1 ounce (30 ml) Cynar (see Resources, page 170)

1 ounce (30 ml) unsweetened 100 percent cranberry juice, chilled

½ to 1 ounce (15 to 30 ml) Vanilla Simple Syrup (page 29)

2 ounces (60 ml) prosecco, chilled

1 ounce (30 ml) soda water, chilled

Orange peel, for garnish (see page 35)

Skewer of 3 green olives, for garnish (see page 37)

Fill a wineglass three-quarters full with ice. Pour the sherry, Cynar, cranberry juice, simple syrup, and prosecco over the ice. Top with the soda water and gently stir to combine. Twist the orange peel over the drink and drop it in. Garnish with the olive skewer.

CARAMEL APPLE SPRITZ

The perfect way to celebrate fall

So easy to make and so delicious, this smooth and easy autumnal spritz pairs the bright juiciness of apple cider with the rich caramelly flavor of Carpano Antica sweet vermouth. If you have it, a drizzle of cinnamon syrup would be an unnecessary but thoroughly delicious addition.

MAKES 1

1½ ounces (45 ml) sweet vermouth, such as Carpano Antica Formula or Punt e Mes (see Resources, page 171)

2 ounces (60 ml) prosecco, chilled

2 ounces (60 ml) sparkling apple cider, chilled

A few dashes of orange bitters (see Resources, page 169)

Apple fan, for garnish (see page 35)

Fill a wineglass three-quarters full with ice. Pour the vermouth, prosecco, and sparkling apple cider over the ice. Gently stir to combine. Add the bitters and garnish with the apple fan.

VARIATION
For an almost zero-proof drink, fill a wineglass three-quarters full with ice. Combine 3 ounces (90 ml) sparkling apple cider with 3 ounces (90 ml) Lurisia chinotto (see Resources, page 169) over the ice. Add ¼ ounce (7 ml) Vanilla Simple Syrup (page 29) and a squeeze of lemon, or more to taste. Add bitters and garnish as directed.

AUTUMN LEAVES

Cozy up by the fire.

Mezcal adds a lovely light and smoky note that makes this spritz reminiscent of sipping cider by a backyard firepit. Blended scotch like Johnnie Walker Black works too, though it results in a stronger, spicier flavored drink. To get plenty of rich apple flavor, go with fresh-pressed apple cider instead of sparkling cider. I love the aromatic piney-floral notes the fresh bay leaf garnish adds, but if you only have dried, skip it.

MAKES 1

2 ounces (60 ml) fresh-pressed apple cider, chilled

1 ounce (30 ml) mezcal or blended scotch

3 ounces (90 ml) ginger beer, preferably Q Mixers (see Resources, page 170), chilled

Thinly sliced apple or apple fan, or dried apple slice, for garnish (see page 35)

Fresh bay leaf, for garnish

Fill a wineglass three-quarters full with ice. Pour the apple cider, mezcal, and ginger beer over the ice. Gently stir to combine and garnish with the apple and bay leaf.

VARIATION

For a zero-proof drink, fill a wineglass three-quarters full with ice. Combine 2 ounces (60 ml) apple cider, 1½ ounces (45 ml) cold lapsang souchong tea, and 2 ounces (60 ml) ginger beer over the ice. Gently stir to combine and garnish as directed.

CENTRAL PARK IN FALL

A maple-y, Manhattan-inspired spritz

Here the classic Manhattan ratio of two parts whiskey, one part sweet vermouth gets turned on its head. A little maple syrup (aged in a bourbon barrel, of course) and sparkling apple cider are added to the mix to give the drink plenty of autumnal flair.

MAKES 1

1 ounce (30 ml) sweet vermouth, such as Carpano Antica Formula or Punt e Mes (see Resources, page 171)

½ ounce (15 ml) bourbon

¼ ounce (7 ml) maple syrup, preferably bourbon barrel–aged maple syrup (see Resources, page 172)

2 ounces (60 ml) prosecco, chilled

2 ounces (60 ml) sparkling apple cider, chilled

A few dashes of orange bitters (see Resources, page 169)

Orange half-wheel, for garnish (see page 37)

Fill a wineglass three-quarters full with ice. Pour the vermouth, bourbon, maple syrup, prosecco, and sparkling apple cider over the ice. Gently stir to combine. Add the bitters and tuck the orange half-wheel between the ice and the side of the glass.

SLEIGHER

Jack Frost doesn't stand a chance.

Red and fizzy and boozy and bitter, this wintry, citrusy spritz is just the ticket to warm you up from the inside. It also works great with a light and spicy ginger beer instead of the prosecco and tonic water or just the tonic water.

MAKES 1

1 ounce (30 ml) Aperol or Campari
(see Resources, page 170)

1 ounce (30 ml) bourbon
(or blended Scotch, or half-and-half)

1 ounce (30 ml) pomegranate juice

¾ ounce (20 ml) fresh orange juice

2 ounces (60 ml) prosecco, chilled

2 ounces (60 ml) tonic water, chilled

Dash of Peychaud's bitters
(see Resources, page 169)

Orange peel, for garnish
(see page 35)

Fill a large wineglass three-quarters full with ice. Pour the Aperol, bourbon, pomegranate juice, orange juice, and prosecco over the ice. Top with the tonic water. Gently stir to combine. Add the bitters. Twist the orange peel over the drink and drop it in.

VARIATION

For an almost zero-proof drink, omit the bourbon. Replace the Aperol with Crodino (see Resources, page 169) and replace the prosecco with ginger beer.

FIGGY PUDDING

Fig jam shakes up into a luscious base for a wintry sipper.

Adding jam to a spritz might seem odd, but it works, especially with the Bonal for structure and Aperol and citrus for brightness. This drink tastes like sticky toffee pudding but in a light and fizzy, highly drinkable form. For a boozier drink, add 1 ounce (30 ml) bourbon to the cocktail shaker before shaking.

MAKES 1

1½ ounces (45 ml) Bonal Gentiane-Quina aperitif (see Resources, page 171)

½ ounce (15 ml) Aperol (see Resources, page 170)

½ ounce (15 ml) fresh lemon juice

½ ounce (15 ml) fresh orange juice

2 tablespoons fig jam, preferably Dalmatia fig spread (see Resources, page 172)

2 ounces (60 ml) prosecco, chilled

2 ounces (60 ml) soda water, chilled

½ dried or fresh fig skewered on a rosemary sprig, for garnish (see page 36)

In a cocktail shaker, combine the Bonal, Aperol, lemon juice, orange juice, and jam. Add a small handful of ice and shake vigorously for about 10 seconds to emulsify the jam into the liquids. Fill a wineglass three-quarters full with ice. Strain the mixture over the ice. Add the prosecco and top with the soda water. Gently stir to combine. Garnish with the fig and rosemary skewer.

VARIATION

For a zero-proof drink, mix 1½ tablespoons fig jam with ½ ounce (15 ml) lemon juice and ½ ounce (15 ml) orange juice in a mixing glass. Fill a wineglass three-quarters full with ice. Strain the mixture over the ice and top with 2 ounces (60 ml) Lurisia chinotto (see Resources, page 169) and 2 to 3 ounces (60 to 90 ml) tonic water. Gently stir. Add 5 drops of high-quality balsamic vinegar. Garnish as directed.

PEAR TREE

Juicy pear cider and woodsy spices

Cynar adds a caramelly bite to juicy pear cider, while a splash of chai concentrate echoes its tannins and adds warm autumn spices. I like to use Bhakti unsweetened chai concentrate because it's widely available and deeply spiced. Rekorderlig pear cider from Sweden is my go-to for this because it has tons of juicy pear flavor. A drier pear cider also works, if you want to enhance the bitterness of the Cynar.

MAKES 1

1½ ounces (45 ml) Cynar
(see Resources, page 170)

1 ounce (30 ml) unsweetened or lightly sweetened chai concentrate (see Resources, page 172)

½ ounce (15 ml) fresh lemon juice

3 ounces (90 ml) pear hard cider, preferably Rekorderlig (see Resources, page 170), chilled

¼ ounce (7 ml) Rosemary Simple Syrup (page 29), or to taste (optional)

Thinly sliced pear or pear fan, for garnish (see page 35)

Fill a wineglass three-quarters full with ice. Pour the Cynar, chai concentrate, lemon juice, and pear hard cider over the ice. Gently stir to combine. Taste and adjust the flavor with a little simple syrup, if desired. Garnish with the pear.

VARIATION
For a zero-proof drink, replace the Cynar with Lurisia chinotto (see Resources, page 169) and replace the hard cider with sparkling apple or pear cider.

FLU FIGHTER

The holy trinity of lemon, ginger, and honey

I love a hot toddy on a cold night, but there's no reason the flavors can't be translated into a fizzy refresher. The only trouble is it's a lot easier to drink more of them. At least the lemon juice adds some all-important vitamin C, and the ginger and cayenne warm you up from the inside.

MAKES 1

1 ounce (30 ml) bourbon
(or Scotch or brandy)

1 ounce (30 ml) fresh lemon juice

½ ounce (15 ml) Honey Simple Syrup
(page 30), plus more (optional)
to taste

¼ teaspoon grated fresh ginger,
or to taste

Pinch of cayenne

3 ounces (90 ml) tonic water
or soda water, chilled

Lemon wheel, for garnish
(see page 37)

Fill a wineglass three-quarters full with ice. Pour the bourbon, lemon juice, and simple syrup over the ice. Add the ginger and cayenne and stir. Top with the tonic water and gently stir to combine. Taste and add more simple syrup, if desired (especially if using Scotch or brandy). Tuck the lemon wheel between the ice and the side of the glass.

VARIATION
For a zero-proof drink, omit the bourbon.

Party-Perfect Spritzes for Any Time of Year

No matter what the season or celebration, there's a world of liqueurs, juices, herbs, and flowers just waiting to be fizzed up. Think seasonally and you can't go wrong. What follows are some go-to flavor combos and the drinks they inspired, but spritzes, in general, are exceptionally easy to batch up in party-ready quantities. If another drink tickles your fancy, just mix the nonfizzy ingredients together, multiply by the number of servings you want to make, and refrigerate. When ready to serve, combine with the requisite amount of bubbles in a pitcher, pour over ice, and garnish.

Fall Feasts: Cranberry juice, apple cider, rosemary and thyme, and amaretto—*The Big Bird* (page 132), *The Nutcracker* (page 135), and Autumn Leaves (page 138)

Winter Parties: Citrus, rosemary and thyme, baking spices, and ginger—*Va-Va-Vermouth* (page 118), *Caramel Apple Spritz* (page 136), and Sweet Thistle (page 121)

Spring Brunch: Lavender, rose, violet, and lemon—*Apercot* (page 79), *The Rosé Garden* (page 63), and French Spritz (page 58)

Summer Soirées: Stone fruits, berries, oranges, melons, and tropical flavors—*Sangria Spritz* (page 86), *Yacht Rock* (page 108), and The Starburst (page 104)

RED FLANNEL ROBE

Chai spices add a cozy glow to tart cranberry.

Garnet-hued cranberry juice is such a natural for winter spritzes. The fruit is in season, the color is holiday themed, and the bright, tart flavor livens up the dreariest days. Here the sweet baking spices of chai concentrate—namely cinnamon, cardamom, and ginger—add warmth, while the black tea, tonic water, and simple syrup balance out the bitter and sweet notes. Unsweetened cranberry juice has the richest flavor, and using unsweetened chai concentrate means you can control the sweetness of the drink with simple syrup. If using sweetened concentrate and cranberry juice cocktail, use the lesser amount of simple syrup. Though it's as easy and comforting as throwing on your favorite robe, this is a great one to batch up for a party.

MAKES 1

1½ ounces (45 ml) unsweetened 100 percent cranberry juice or cranberry juice cocktail, chilled

1 ounce (30 ml) unsweetened or lightly sweetened chai concentrate (see Resources, page 172), chilled

¼ to ½ ounce (7 to 15 ml) Simple Syrup (page 28)

3 ounces (90 ml) tonic water, chilled

Rosemary sprig, for garnish (see page 36)

Fill a wineglass three-quarters full with ice. Pour the cranberry juice, chai concentrate, simple syrup, and tonic water over the ice. Gently stir to combine and garnish with the rosemary sprig.

A GUIDE TO THE COMPONENTS

There's no limit to the ingredients you can use when concocting a spritz. Nearly anything at the liquor store is fair game, not to mention the supermarket produce aisle and cold drinks case. Here you will find a brief guide to the liqueurs, vermouths, spirits, wines, and mixers that the recipes in this book were built on. Once you familiarize yourself with these ingredients, it'll be even easier to start riffing on your own.

Amari, Other Liqueurs, and Vermouths

CITRUSY

Aperol

Bright orange and sweet, Aperol is far less bitter than Campari, and its citrus flavor is a bit more grapefruity and less herbal. It originated in Padua, near Venice, where the Aperol spritz was born.

Campari

It looks almost identical to Aperol, but Campari packs a big bitter orange punch, thanks to a generous infusion of gentian root. The bitterness can be an acquired taste for some. Campari was first developed in Milan, and used as the base for Negroni and Americano cocktails.

Cappelletti Aperitivo Americano

Cappelletti is wine-based and flat-out delicious even on its own. A heady dose of vanilla rounds out the bitter orange and grapefruit notes, making this a great choice if palate-slapping bitterness isn't your thing.

Limoncello

There doesn't seem to be one way to make this bittersweet lemon liqueur. Some brands are very sweet, some almost herbal. I go with Pallini since it's good quality and easy to find, but do some sleuthing to find one you like. Even better, make it yourself (see page 93).

FLORAL

Crème de Violette

If you're a fan of the Aviation cocktail, you might already have a bottle of this on hand. If not, it's a great addition to your bar if you love floral flavors. Note that it's intense, bordering on perfumed soap, but in small doses it adds gorgeous lavender color and violet-blossom flavor, which goes exceptionally well with New Western–style botanical gins such as Thinking Tree (see page 172).

Lillet Blanc

Lillet tastes like a bright and juicy white wine mixed with floral honey and a touch of bitter botanicals. Its lush sweetness mixes perfectly into spritzes with fresh summer fruit. The French aperitif is wine-based and infused with quinine, which gives it the requisite bitter notes to keep things refreshing.

St-Germain

This French elderflower liqueur tastes like honey and is just as versatile. Once you pick up a bottle, you'll find yourself adding it to all sorts of cocktails.

HERBAL

Cocchi Americano Bianco

An aromatized wine, Cocchi Americano is herbal and citrusy, but with a sweet backdrop of golden raisins. When concocting something light and fruity that needs a bit of structure, reach for this.

Mattei Cap Corse Blanc

This Corsican aromatized wine is similar to a white vermouth, but it's infused with cinchona bark (which contains quinine) instead of wormwood. It's also a bit sweeter. But take a whiff and you'll be bowled over by an almost savory, vegetal, saline minerality. The flavor, however, is completely different, more of a complexly herbal citrus-fennel combo. It's great for enhancing any green and grassy flavors.

Suze

Bright yellow Suze is rather new to the States but a longtime favorite aperitif of the French. It's usually served on the rocks or with a splash of soda or tonic, but these days Suze is finding its way into a surprising range of cocktails. This earthy bitter liqueur goes with everything from berry flavors to dark cocoa notes. It gets its bitterness from gentian root, just like Campari does. It's kind of like Campari if you swapped out the orange for a bunch of herbs, which is how Suze came to be the cornerstone of the White Negroni.

Yellow Chartreuse

This liqueur from the French Alps is made with 130 plants and flowers. As complex as it sounds, it's actually quite approachable—sweet and honeyed with distinct floral, citrus, and anise notes. The original Green Chartreuse is bolder and boozier, herbaceous and minty. Both kinds of Chartreuse seem to be having a moment, getting play in more cocktails in the States these days. If you have room on your bar cart for even a half bottle, it's really fun to play with.

NUTTY

Amaretto

This sweet almond Italian liqueur is not only a great addition to coffee, but it also goes gorgeously with stone fruits, holiday spices, and even tiki drinks in place of orgeat—a perishable almond-and-orange-blossom syrup that most people (except for tiki enthusiasts) don't usually have on hand. When you want your spritz to have a little nutty roundness, splash in a smidge of amaretto.

Sherry (Amontillado or Oloroso)

Spain's famed sherry is essentially oxidized wine, and the longer it ages, the more deliciously nutty it tastes. The extra-aged oloroso variety is famous for its rich almond-toffee and dried-fruit notes, and it's fortified with a bit of alcohol too, giving it a stronger flavor. It's great in holiday-spiced spritzes, as is the comparatively lighter but similarly nutty amontillado sherry.

RICH, SPICED, AND BITTERSWEET

Averna

This Sicilian amaro has the rich smoothness and intriguing herbal notes of a sweet vermouth, but it's richer and more bitter with overt orange flavors and a touch of licorice and rosemary. Amari Meletti and Ramazzotti both have a similar flavor profile with a pronounced cola flavor.

Bonal Gentiane-Quina

This tastes like grown-up cherry cola. A fortified wine from near the French Alps, it's lightly bittersweet with tons of burnt-sugar, cherry, and dried-fruit flavors, with a touch of anise.

Cynar

If you see the artichoke on the label and think this will be some kind of weird vegetal concoction, think again. Although Cynar is indeed made with artichoke leaves (and a dozen other plants), this amaro tastes deliciously of burnt sugar with distinct floral notes. When you want to add a honey-like sweetness with a wallop of bitterness to a spritz, think Cynar.

Sweet Vermouth

Typically, sweet vermouths are red-wine based, with caramelly notes that pair well with brown spirits. They have enough going on that they can easily stand alone in a spritz or complement one made with a splash of bourbon or Campari. Carpano Antica Formula is one of the best and most widely available. Punt e Mes, another favorite, is slightly richer and more bitter. Cocchi Vermouth di Torino has a spiciness that works well in a wide range of drinks. Mattei

Cap Corse Rouge is another deliciously bitter option. The fortified and aromatized wine isn't technically a vermouth because it's made with cinchona bark instead of wormwood, but that's just splitting hairs. Bottom line: Explore the wide world of red vermouths and find your own favorite, then give it the spritz treatment.

Sparkling Wine

Cava

This category of Spanish wine is incredibly cheap considering it must be made in the méthode champenoise style like Champagne. That means each bottle has to be inoculated with yeast for the secondary fermentation to produce the bubbles, and that's just one step in the labor-intensive process (though nowadays it's mostly mechanized). A bottle of good Cava will taste more like Champagne than prosecco does—with toasty, yeasty notes and similarly fine bubbles. But a good Cava costs around $10, whereas a good (not even great!) Champagne costs closer to $40. The grapes used are different, of course. Macabeo, Parellada, and Xarel-lo are the three main grapes used for Cava, which produce its signature "lemony pears with a touch of almond" taste profile. Cava with the word *riserva* on the label is aged longer, giving it more yeasty notes. Again, go for a brut if you want very little sweetness, or extra-dry if you want just a touch more.

Champagne/Sparkling Wine

To be called Champagne, the wine must be made in the Champagne region of France from mainly Chardonnay, Pinot Noir, and Pinot Meunier grapes and produced using the méthode champenoise process. If it doesn't satisfy all these requirements, it's a sparkling wine. That means a sparkling wine made with the same method from the same varietal of grapes but grown in,

say, Napa, may taste like a fine Champagne and cost as much but isn't technically Champagne. So don't get hung up on the name. If you like the fine bubbles and notes of toasted brioche and citrus zest typical of French Champagne, feel free to explore any sparkling wine made with those iconic grapes. Keep in mind that anything made with premium grapes like Chardonnay and Pinot Noir usually has a high price tag. And if it's made in the labor-intensive méthode champenoise style, that adds to the price too. As with any other sparkler intended for a spritz, brut is usually best.

Lambrusco

One of the oldest styles of wines made in Italy, Lambrusco is a light, juicy, and fruity sparkling red wine. Its fruitiness is fabulous in the Sangria Spritz (page 86). There are over sixty grape varietals that can comprise Lambrusco, but of those, six are the most typically used. Look for the DOC (denominazione di origine controllata) label, which is your clue that it will be a quality

wine from one of the eight best growing regions. It comes in both sweet (dolce) and dry (brut) styles. Definitely opt for brut when using it for spritzes.

Pét-Nat

Short for the French term *pétillant naturel*, pét-nats are natural sparkling wines that have exploded in popularity in recent years, mainly because they're fun, affordable, and always a surprise. They're made with the age-old méthode ancestrale technique, which likely started as an "oops" centuries ago. Essentially, wines are bottled before they're fully fermented and get their fizz in the bottle as the remaining sugars convert to alcohol and produce carbon dioxide. As a result, you never truly know what a pét-nat is going to taste like until you open it. Pét-nats can be made with any varietal of grape, in any style (red, white, pink, orange), and are usually a bit cloudy and fizzy rather than bubbly. Some are super juicy; some are bone dry. Whether pét-nats work in a spritz depends only on your own taste preferences; I think they open up a world of possibilities. Pét-nats are made in wine regions around the world, not just France. If you want to stay true to the Italian tradition of spritzes and still get a taste of these wild wonders, look for prosecco col fondo. *Col fondo* means "with the bottom," which refers to the sediment at the bottom of the bottle.

Prosecco

This Italian wine is made mostly with the Glera (aka Prosecco) grape varietal that's grown mainly in northern Italy's Veneto region. It gets its bubbles from secondary fermentation in tanks (called the Charmat method), which generally makes it more affordable than sparkling wines that get their secondary fermentation in the bottle (the méthode champenoise). Tank fermentation also means the wine doesn't spend as much time in contact with lees (expended yeast cells) and builds up about half the pressure. As a result, prosecco tends to be fruity rather than yeasty, and less fizzy than Champagne. Personally, I think prosecco's fruity, honey notes are ideal for balancing the bitter liqueurs in spritzes. Keep in mind, sparkling wines that are made using the Charmat method tend to have bigger, looser bubbles that fade a bit faster than the bubbles in wines made using the méthode champenoise. The bubbles in force-carbonated wines fade even faster. Like other sparkling wines, prosecco comes in a range of sweetness levels. Opt for a dry (aka brut) wine if you want to control the sweetness of your spritz.

If you have a Costco membership, you're in luck. One of the most affordable and high-quality prosecco options around is Kirkland Signature Asolo Prosecco Superiore at $7 a bottle. This is an extra-dry wine, so it's a bit sweeter than a brut, but I find it's not that much sweeter and still works great in a spritz. It's made in one of the best growing areas in the Veneto region and has the highest classification of Italian wines (DOCG, or denominazione di origine controllata e garantita).

Sparkling Rosé

Sparkling rosés can be inexpensive, fruit-forward, fizzy red and white wine blends blasted with carbon dioxide and sealed in a can, or they can be spare, elegant méthode champenoise wines made exclusively from Pinot Noir grapes crushed to allow the juice and skin to mingle for a controlled amount of time. Clearly, there's going to be a huge range of potential flavor notes when it comes to rosé. For a spritz, go with the inexpensive option. Sparkling rosé works great when you want to infuse the spritz with more rosy pink color and a more overtly fruity flavor. When deciding what to buy, pay attention to the tasting notes on the label and choose a rosé with flavors and aromas that will pair well with the other ingredients in your spritz.

Spirits

Bourbon, Rye, and Scotch

The warm, woodsy, toffee, and vanilla notes of bourbon go great with any spritz that's sporting warm flavors, sweet vermouths, or caramelly amari. Rye whiskey adds spicy-savory notes instead. Scotch is a lot smokier, so it tends to overpower. But a well-balanced scotch, like Johnnie Walker Black, works well anywhere you want a hint of smoky spice.

Jamaican Rum

The world of rum is so huge and varied, there's no way to single out just one type to keep around. A well-stocked bar cart always has bottles of spiced, dark, overproof, white, and amber rum, because each works best in different drinks. But if you're looking for versions that tend to be complex and interesting, go for a Jamaican rum. They just have a lot going on. Appleton Estate (see Resources, page 170) is a bartender favorite. A little Jamaican rum goes a long way, which is perfect for keeping the ABV low in tiki-style spritzes.

Mezcal

The smoky qualities of mezcal add depth to drinks without overpowering them, and spritzes are no exception. Mezcal provides a clean hint of smoke, like how the air smells when the neighbors have their fireplaces going, rather than the in-your-face smoke of a peaty scotch.

New Western Gin

Many of the floral spritzes in this book get their backbone from a splash of gin rather than the typical amari, which are just too bold to let the floral flavors come through. Keep in mind, however, that the typical juniper-forward London dry is not the ideal choice for a floral spritz. Instead, you want a newfangled "Western" gin that goes all in on other herbs and spices too. Look for one that specifically aims for floral notes. My favorite is Thinking Tree gin from Eugene, Oregon (see Resources, page 172). **For a zero-proof way to add gin-like flavor to drinks, Seedlip brand (see Resources, page 171) is easy to find these days, and the Garden 108 version is bursting with botanical flavor.**

Tequila

Just a splash of tequila adds a little warmth to citrusy spritzes. Opt for the clean flavor of silver tequila and always one made with 100 percent agave.

Mix-Ins

Beer

There's only one beer spritz in this book (page 97), but it's really just the beginning. If you're a beer lover, give yourself permission to play around and see what a wallop of hops can add to a spritz. Juicy IPAs, especially those with lots of grapefruity citrus notes like the ones from Cascade, Citra, and Amarillo hops, work exceptionally well with citrusy amari like Campari and Aperol.

Bitters

There's hardly any drink that can't be improved by a dash of

bitters. They're made of clear alcohol infused with all kinds of bitter botanicals. I lean toward highly aromatic options with lots of spices or citrus oils. A few dashes and suddenly your spritz has a lot more dimension. Try using Fee Brothers orange or grapefruit bitters (see Resources, page 169) in citrusy spritzes, and Angostura or Peychaud's (see Resources, page 169) in tropical or holiday spritzes that can take the hint of spice. **Although a few drops of bitters won't affect the ABV of the drink, you should skip them if you want it completely alcohol-free.**

Ginger Beer

The spiciness of ginger works well with so many flavors—from stone fruits, citrus, and coconut to spirits like bourbon, scotch, and tequila—that it can be hard to resist adding ginger to every spritz. That said, most ginger ales are too weak to stand out in a spritz, and more intense ginger beers are a bit too sweet. An amaro or liqueur adds plenty of sweetness on its own, and when you essentially add soda

pop, even a gingery one, it's a bit too much. The best I've found is Q Mixers ginger beer (see Resources, page 170), which has a great spicy kick without the syrup factor. Q Mixers also makes a light version. When even that is too sweet, opt for soda water and grated fresh ginger instead.

Ice

A spritz doesn't need fancy ice, but it does need a lot of it, which is why it's a good idea to take your ice at least somewhat seriously. Ideally, you want ice that tastes good, not freezer-burnt or like chemicals. Consider using filtered water and storing the ice in an airtight container in the freezer. Regular ice cubes are the go-to shape because they won't melt too fast and dilute your drink like crushed ice or bullet ice, which has a hole in the middle. If you really want to geek out on ice, you can make a big batch of clear ice and break it up. Clear ice (as opposed to cloudy ice) has less oxygen trapped in it so it melts far more slowly. Look online for DIY methods and reviews of ice makers. And if you're planning to make more than a few spritzes over the course of a few hours, be sure to keep your ice freezer-cold, not slowly melting in an ice bucket.

Italian Bitter Soda

With any luck, we will soon see the day when the adorable 3-ounce (90 ml) bottles of Sanbittèr and Crodino and the slightly larger ones of Lurisia chinotto are as ubiquitous in the United States as they are in Italy. Until then, you can find them, but you'll have to pay about a dollar an ounce for them at a gourmet market or online (see Resources, pages 169 and 170). They're worth it. These nonalcoholic sodas made with some of the same bittering agents as Italian amari are incredible stand-ins when you want a zero-proof spritz. They're also great on their own poured over ice with an orange peel twisted over the top, or diluted with a bit of soda water, tonic, or lemonade. Crodino is a ringer for Campari's bitter orange flavor. Sanbittèr has more of a sweet cherry-cola flavor with a bitter punch. Lurisia

chinotto is almost like a mix of both—think bitter orange with sweet dried-fruit notes.

Juices

Packaged juices, whether shelf-stable or in the refrigerator section, usually taste cooked—because they are. They're pasteurized with heat, and in the process, they lose their bright and fresh flavor. That's why whenever possible, you should opt for fresh-squeezed juices, especially when it comes to citrus. There's no excuse not to squeeze a lemon, lime, orange, or grapefruit right into the glass, but other fruits are trickier. For apple, look for refrigerated fresh-pressed apple cider, but sparkling cider is light and refreshing enough too. Cranberry and pomegranate are fine from the bottle, but be sure they're uncut with other juices and unsweetened so you can control the sweetness of your drink. You can always add simple syrup (see page 28). For passion fruit, you can get frozen blocks of puree and let them defrost. Dole pineapple juice is pretty unimpeachable, but your spritz will taste even better if you puree fresh pineapple chunks and strain the juice. Watermelon easily works the same way. Stone fruits like peaches and apricots are almost always better muddled in the glass, but not everyone wants a sipper with fruit bits. In that case, high-quality shelf-stable fruit "nectars" from Ceres or Kern's (see Resources, pages 169 and 170) will work, but go easy—too much and you venture into smoothie territory.

Shrubs

These are drink concentrates with centuries-deep roots. Fruit is mashed with sugar and left to macerate, then strained and mixed with cider vinegar for a tart and fruity syrup. These days you can sometimes find bottled shrubs at farmers' markets and premium grocery stores, but you can't beat homemade for taste and freshness. (See pages 32–34 for recipes.)

Soda Pop

If you don't want to add too much additional sugar to your spritzes, stay away from sodas—with a few exceptions. Italian orange sodas, like Sanpellegrino Aranciata (orange) and Aranciata Rossa (blood orange) have a bold citrus tang that can make bitter spritzes deliciously palatable for the uninitiated without making them sickly sweet. Do not try to substitute orange sodas like Fanta; they're far too sweet with no bite. Dry Soda Company (see Resources, page 169) offers a lineup that works well at adding flavor and fizz without the syrupy sweetness of traditional soda. The vanilla, lavender, and cucumber are my favorites.

Syrups

Simple syrup (equal parts sugar and water) is essential for calibrating the sweetness of a drink, and although plain simple syrup is infinitely useful, you can infuse it with all kinds of herbs and spices. Don't be tempted at the supermarket by flavored syrups, which are usually extremely sweet and made with artificial flavors. It's easy to make your own syrups; see pages 28–31 for recipes.

Tonic Water

This quinine-infused water is delightfully bitter—ideal for adding backbone to spritzes that forgo an amaro or use very little of it. But tonic water is also sweet. Opt for brands with the least sugar so you don't end up with a too-sweet drink, especially when mixing booze-free spritzes made with generous amounts of juices and syrups. Q Mixers Spectacular tonic water is lower in sugar than most other brands, and they make a light version too.

Fever-Tree Refreshingly Light Indian tonic water is another great choice (see Resources, page 170). The regular version is a favorite too; just keep in mind, it makes for a slightly sweeter drink. In addition to the quinine and sugar, some brands will add a variety of other ingredients or spices to shake things up—Q Mixers has an elderflower tonic that I adore in spare, floral spritzes—so keep the sweetness and those flavors in mind when playing around.

GLOSSARY

If you're looking for liqueurs to spritzify or want to make a substitution in one of the recipes in this book, it helps to be familiar with the verbiage that differentiates them. Here are a few of the terms you're likely to come across, and what they mean.

amaro (plural: amari): An Italian bitter liqueur (*amar* means "bitter"), usually made with a neutral spirit and a multitude of fruits, flowers, herbs, and bittering agents. Some amari, such as Campari, are considered an aperitivo, meant to be sipped before dinner to prime the palate for the meal to come. Some, such as Cynar, are more traditionally a digestivo, meant to be sipped alone after dinner to aid digestion, although it's just as natural to mix them with soda water and sip them during the day.

Americano: Considered a subcategory of quinquina, this fortified and aromatized wine (such as Cocchi Americano) has gentian root, which is an intense bittering agent. The name refers to its bitterness (*amaricante* means "bittered"), and some say it plays on what was an old American tourist tradition of adding bitters to vermouth.

aperitivo: An Italian term for a predinner drink and usually a snack too. In France, you'd order an aperitif instead.

chinato/quinquina: A category of fortified and aromatized wine like vermouth, but primarily infused with cinchona bark—which is what the quinine often used in tonic water comes from—rather than wormwood. Chinatos are Italian, and those made with Barolo are prized and expensive. Quinquina (such as Cap Corse and Lillet) are typically French.

digestivo: An Italian term for an after-dinner drink, usually a straight shot of amaro. In France, you'd order a digestif instead.

vermouth: Red or white wine fortified (usually with brandy) and aromatized with infusions of herbs, spices, and bark. To be considered vermouth, it must be infused with wormwood. Red vermouth is typically sweeter and heavier than white, which is typically dry.

RESOURCES

Books

Amaro: The Spirited World of Bittersweet, Herbal Liqueurs, with Cocktails, Recipes, and Formulas, by Brad Thomas Parsons

The Bar Book: Elements of Cocktail Technique, by Jeffrey Morgenthaler with Martha Holmberg

Spritz: Italy's Most Iconic Aperitivo Cocktail, with Recipes, by Talia Baiocchi and Leslie Pariseau

Ingredients

BITTERS

Fee Brothers
feebrothers.com
Grapefruit and West Indian Orange
   bitters

The House of Angostura
angosturabitters.com
Angostura aromatic bitters

Sazerac
sazerac.com
Peychaud's bitters

SODA AND MIXERS

Ceres
ceresjuices.com
Tropical fruit juices

Crodino
crodino.com
Crodino Italian soda

Dry Soda Company
drinkdry.com
Vanilla, cucumber, and lavender
   sparkling sodas

Eataly
eataly.com
Lurisia chinotto, balsamic vinegar of
   Modena DOP or IGP

169

Fever-Tree
fever-tree.com
Elderflower and Refreshingly Light
Premium Indian tonic waters

Kern's
kerns.com
Apricot nectar and other fruit juices

Q Mixers
qmixers.com
Ginger beer, tonic water, and
elderflower tonic water

Rekorderlig
rekorderlig.com
Pear hard cider

R.W. Knudsen Family
rwknudsenfamily.com
Sparkling cherry juice

Sanpellegrino
sanpellegrinofruitbeverages.com
Aranciata soda, Aranciata Rossa
soda, and Sanbittèr soda

Spindrift
drinkspindrift.com
Lemon- and grapefruit-infused
sparkling waters

Topo Chico
topochicousa.net
Soda water

Waterloo
drinkwaterloo.com
Coconut and other flavored
sparkling waters

SPIRITS

Appleton Estate
appletonestate.com/en
Eight-year-old reserve Jamaican rum

Astor Wines & Spirits
astorwines.com
Suze aperitif

Averna
amaroaverna.com
Amaro Averna Siciliano

Barbadillo
fells.co.uk/our-producers/barbadillo
Oloroso and amontillado sherry

Bulleit
bulleit.com
Bourbon and rye

Campari Group
camparigroup.com
Aperol, Campari, and Cynar

Cappelletti
cappellettinovasalus.it/eng
Cappelletti Aperitivo Americano

Carpano
carpano.com/en/prodotto/antica
 -formula-2
Carpano Antica Formula and Punt e
Mes Italian sweet vermouths

Chartreuse
chartreuse.fr/en/produits/yellow
 -chartreuse
Yellow and Green Chartreuse

Cocchi
cocchi.it/en/wines/americano
Cocchi Americano Bianco, Cocchi
 Rosa, Cocchi Storico Vermouth di
 Torino

Del Maguey
delmaguey.com
Vida mezcal

Dolin
dolin.fr/en/products/bonal
Blanc vermouth, Bonal Gentiane-
 Quina

Espolòn
espolontequila.com/blanco
Tequila blanco

G'Vine
g-vine.com/en
Floraison French floral gin

Haus Alpenz
alpenz.com
Mattei Cap Corse Blanc and Rouge,
 Rothman & Winter crème de
 violette

Johnnie Walker
johnniewalker.com/en-us
Black Label Scotch whisky

Lillet
lillet.com/en
Lillet Blanc

Lyre's
lyres.com
Italian Orange nonalcoholic spirit

Ninkasi Brewing Company
ninkasibrewing.com
Prismatic Juicy IPA

Pallini
limoncellopallini.com
Limoncello

Seedlip
seedlipdrinks.com/en-us
Garden 108 distilled nonalcoholic
 spirit

St-Germain
stgermain.fr/us/en
Elderflower liqueur

Thinking Tree Spirits
thinkingtreespirits.com
Gifted Gin

Woodford Reserve
woodfordreserve.com
Bourbon

SYRUPS AND MIX-INS
Crown Maple
crownmaple.store
Bourbon barrel-aged maple syrup

Dalmatia
dalmatiaspreads.com
Fig spread

D'Arbo
darbo.at/en/products/syrup
Elderflower syrup

IKEA
ikea.com
*Dryck Fläder (elderflower drink
concentrate)*

Tazah
mideastgrocers.com/products
/tazah-rose-syrup-500ml
Rose syrup

**TEA, SPICES, AND DRIED
FLOWERS**
Bhakti Chai
drinkbhakti.com
*Unsweetened and lightly sweetened
chai concentrate*

Diaspora Co.
diasporaco.com
Single-origin ground turmeric

The Jasmine Pearl
thejasminepearl.com
*Loose-leaf rose petals, lavender
buds, hibiscus tea, green tea*

Tools

Crate & Barrel
crateandbarrel.com
*Cocktail shakers, mixing glasses,
muddlers, strainers, Champagne
stopper, glassware*

OXO
oxo.com

*Wooden citrus reamer, small citrus
juicer, mini measuring beaker set,
Y vegetable peelers*

World Market
worldmarket.com
Bamboo cocktail skewers

ACKNOWLEDGMENTS

Writing a cookbook is both a joy and a huge undertaking, and I couldn't have done it without the incredible support (and brutal honesty) of my husband, Mike, and my resident cheerleaders (and best daughters ever), Emma and Audrey. I can't wait until you're old enough to sip spritzes with me in the Cinque Terre. Big thanks to photographer Eric Medsker for bringing the recipes to life so beautifully. And I'm deeply grateful to Lia Ronnen and Judy Pray for entrusting me with this project, to Shoshana Gutmajer and Elise Ramsbottom for careful editing and smart insights every step of the way, and to the entire Artisan team who worked so hard to make the book better than I could have ever dreamed: Suet Chong, Nina Simoneaux, Sibylle Kazeroid, Barbara Peragine, Nancy Murray, Donna G. Brown, Allison McGeehon, Theresa Collier, Amy Kattan Michelson, and Patrick Thedinga.

INDEX

Note: Page numbers in *italics* refer to illustrations.

DANIELLE CENTONI is a James Beard Award-winning food writer and cookbook author based in Portland, Oregon. In her two-decade career, she has worked as a staff editor and writer for the *Oakland Tribune*, the *Oregonian*, *Imbibe* magazine, *Mix* magazine, and Eater Portland. She is the author of several books, including *Portland Cooks* and *Fried Rice*, and has contributed to many others. You can find her work in a wide range of publications and media, including *Better Homes & Gardens*, *EatingWell*, and The Kitchn.